C000215546

CUMBRIAN CONTRASTS
a vision of countryside

CUMBRIAN
CONTRASTS

a vision of countryside

Jan Wiltshire

Locations Explored in *Cumbrian Contrasts*

Wast Water

Windermere

Coniston Water

River Duddon

8

Millom

Ulverston

Grange-Over-Sands

14

9

Barrow-in-Furness

Morecambe Bay

Walney Island

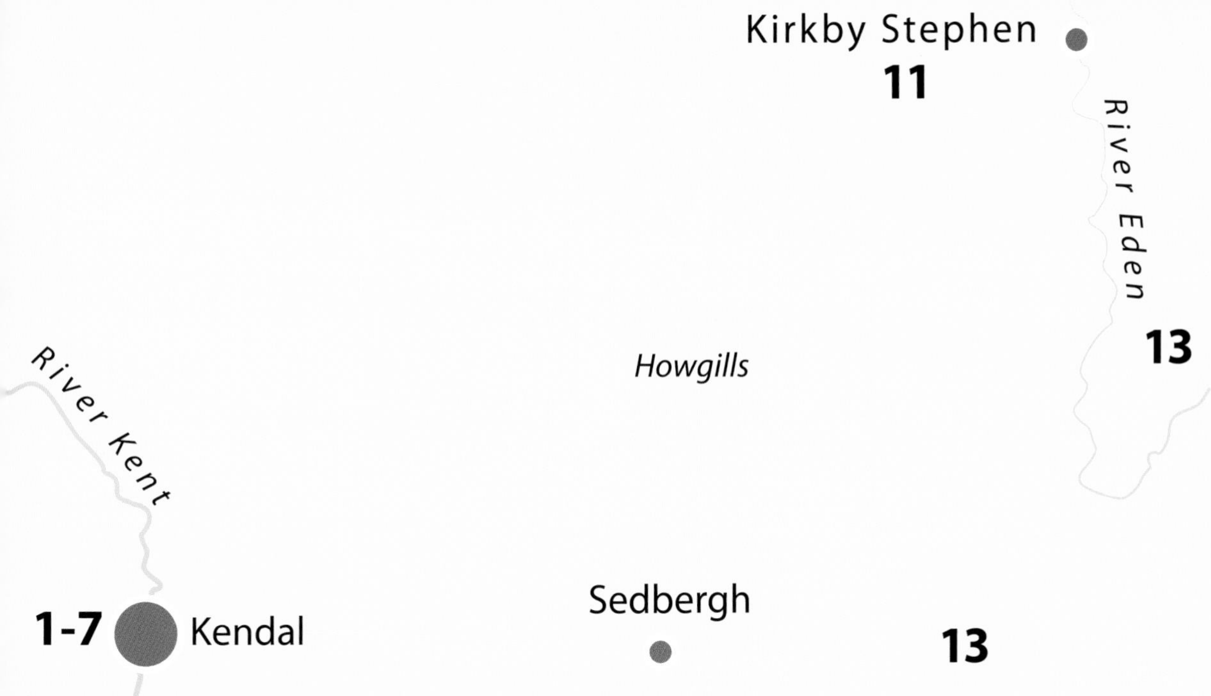

Kirkby Stephen ●
11

River Eden

Howgills

13

River Kent

1-7 ● Kendal

Sedbergh
●

13

10

Contents

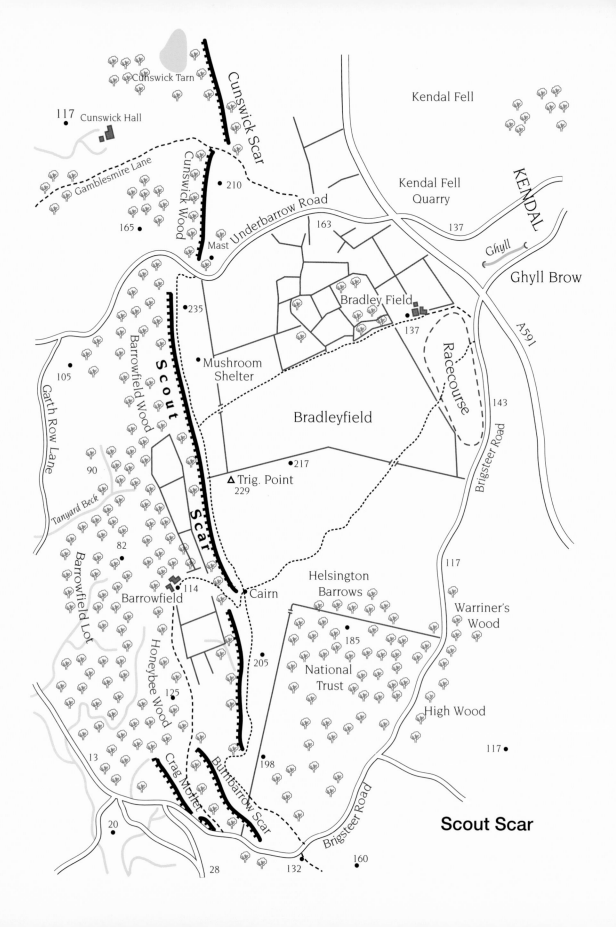

Cunswick Tarn

117 Cunswick Hall

Gamblesmire Lane

165

Cunswick Scar

Cunswick Wood

210

Mast

Underbarrow Road

Kendal Fell

Kendal Fell Quarry

137

KENDAL

Ghyll

Ghyll Brow

A591

163

Bradley Field

137

Racecourse

143

Brigsteer Road

235

105

Garth Row Lane

90

Tanyard Beck

82

Barrowfield Lot

Barrowfield Wood

Scout Scar

Mushroom Shelter

Bradleyfield

217

△ Trig. Point
229

114

Barrowfield

Honeybee Wood

125

13

20

28

Crag Mottet

Barnbarrow Scar

132

205

198

160

Cairn

Helsington Barrows

185

National Trust

117

Warriner's Wood

High Wood

117

Scout Scar

Acknowledgements

My thanks to all who have helped in diverse ways during the
making of *Cumbrian Contrasts*. To The Friends, for the extract from
Stramongate Quaker School magazine of 1906. To Jackie Fey, Local
Studies Librarian, Kendal Library, who drew it to my attention. To Dr
Rob Lambert, tourism and environment academic at The University
of Nottingham for permission to quote from *Shared Planet: Ground
Nesting Birds*. To Liz and Colin Hotchkiss who organised field-trips and
to all reserve wardens who were our guides. When identification of flora
and fauna proves intractable an ecologist friend gives generous and
expert help and consults her specialist colleagues on my behalf.
To family and friends. To Dr Jill Clough, David Hunt, Fiona Holman,
Pauline Brooks, Barbara and Austin Farr, Geoff Brooks and Mike
Dewey. To my publisher Anna Goddard, designer Lucy Frontani and the
team at Carnegie. Any mistakes in this book are ultimately my own.

My love of the natural world is embedded deep and that's what I like
to share. Whilst writing *Cumbrian Contrasts* I've kept a nature writer's
blog on my website:

www.cumbrianaturally.co.uk

Book and blog complement each other and interact. The blog
has become my archive and source material, an opportunity to
experiment. I shall return to locations and themes explored in
Cumbrian Contrasts, taking the story forward into the future.

January 2016

Autumn Gentian
Gentianella amarella

Introduction

AN HOUR AFTER MIDNIGHT twelve children made their way through the town heading for Scout Scar. They left the last of the houses behind;

> 'there burst upon us, all unforeseen, such a 'festival chorus' of larks as no one of us had ever heard before. On all sides, unseen in the gray dimness, they sang as if their little hearts could hold no longer the rising flood of music, and they must needs shake it out anyhow, anywhere, with splendid unthrift, above the gray sleeping world.'*

As the stars faded away they reached the escarpment and waited for sunrise. But lark song was the surprise and wonder of that midsummer morning in 1906.

As a naturalist, my focus is on our experience of countryside, then and now. These children give us a glimpse of how it was. 2014 saw commemorations to mark the centenary of the outbreak of The First World War, 1914–18. Throughout the year in a constant refrain, media coverage reflected on life in Britain a hundred years ago. I wrote the core of *Cumbrian Contrasts* in this context, with a heightened awareness of history.

Late in 2013, extensive building programmes for Kendal and Ulverston were unveiled. Change was imminent. The character of Kendal would change and so would the countryside on its doorstep.

I'd like the children of today and tomorrow to be surprised and delighted by lark song and the call of the cuckoo. I hope that may be part of their experience but both species are in dramatic decline and there's nothing to protect the ground-nesting birds of Scout Scar. *Save the skylark*, that's the watchword. The bird is an emblem of species-loss. For wildlife and countryside everywhere we all have a part to play.

Cumbrian Contrasts celebrates the wonder of the natural world. It's a snapshot in time, a portrait of now that reflects on the past and looks to the future.

Like those children, I walk from Kendal and head for Scout Scar. Venturing beyond, I radiate out across Cumbria excited by the prospect of all I might discover.

*Lucy M. Reynolds, *Sunrise on Scout Scar*, from Stramongate Quaker School Magazine, September 1906.

Kendal

a town with a river at its heart

FURTHER, THAT'S WHERE I SHALL GO, further into the Cumbrian countryside. But I'll begin with the year a top predator came to town. The creature is said to be secretive but if you seek diligently you might glimpse it at dawn or at dusk. This one hadn't read the script.

The river flowed fast and the otter swam upstream, sleek and sinuous. She crunched on something crustacean, showing teeth, whiskers, dense pelt and muscular tail as she surfaced beneath our riverside walk. A photographer came each day from the Wirral and pictured her eating a fish. Her diet would be trout, bullhead or salmon, so information boards suggested. The winter the otter came to Kendal we were all eager to see, to share, to understand.

Daylight appearances and confiding behaviour were odd but made otter watching easier. I listened to tales from the riverbank, eager to hear what this meant to others. They spoke of their relationship with the natural world. A local man lived here in boyhood, close to the river. In the 1950s, he found otter in the tributaries of the Mint and Sprint, but not in the River Kent in town. Our bitch otter was news and, during the winter of 2012/13, she became a tourist attraction. A couple had seen her half an hour ago, opposite the Parish Church. A woman showed me otter prints in the snow below Stramongate Bridge, close to her home. A young father introduced his little girl to her first otter, and told me where he had found kingfisher as a boy. The river held us in a spectrum of time; in reminiscence, in the moment with each glimpse of otter, and here was a gift beyond price for the next generation. This is our river, our inheritance, pass it on.

Something had changed. Wildlife and people tend to lead parallel lives but now we engaged with the life of the river in a spirit of reverence, with a respect for the natural world. Welcome, say those interpretative boards which invite us to consider the ecology of the river and to see what we can find. There was a shopping trolley and a bike in the river but otters don't ride bikes and a river is not a rubbish dump. The idyll is rarely unalloyed but the aura around the otter suggested how things might be, if we could somehow tap into the benevolence that flowed among us.

Through Kendal, the Civic Society has plaques and offers guided walks to draw us into the story of the town. Tourists and locals like to know what's special, what there is to see, whether it's history or natural history, urban or rural. But the storytelling falters as we leave town and head for the countryside.

The catchment of the River Kent is an SSSI, a Site of Special Scientific Interest. So is Scout Scar, but it's not clear what that means and acronyms don't make a story. When we arrive in the countryside we want to know what will make our day. So what are we hoping for as we put on our boots and set forth?

Rue-leaved
Saxifrage
*Saxifraga
tridactylites*

Ghyll Brow

an approach to Scout Scar

WHERE DOES THE COUNTRYSIDE BEGIN? We may not find it tomorrow where we left it yesterday.

Tyre tracks slewed off the road and ploughed into the verge, demolished a pile of grit close to the mossy wall, swerved back to the road and down into town. Hardly a skid on ice in such a mild winter. Perhaps it was youths heading home after a night out, a night out of town, a night in the wilds, that transition zone where town segues into countryside. Litter along the verge told the story; cider bottles and drinks cans, fast-food wrappers and cigarettes. Aluminium cans were shoved into the earth as if they might take root and flower. Sometimes I clear up the mess, sometimes I choose to see only the rural idyll.

From the road, daphne looked darkly evergreen at the top of a steep bank against a mossy wall. This wettest of winters saw the ground saturated but to photograph those early green flowers I had to be up close. High on the bank my footing was precarious and a woman somersaulting down into the Brigsteer Road would have been a novelty. I could have summoned the mountain rescue on one of their sillier calls. Sapling spikes from a brutal flailing snagged at my legs. There were trailing brambles, blackthorn and dog rose; without gloves I couldn't hang onto them and I slithered down the bank and landed at the feet of a woman with a black Labrador.

Those February flowers were almost hidden. 'Honey-scented,' writes Marjorie Blamey in her *Flora*.* Twice up that sodden bank was enough so I took her word for it. They were exquisite flowers to find on a winter's morning. Through spring and summer it's a joy to follow the sequence

Forget-me-not in fog

of flowers with something new to discover each day. Until 8 June 2015 when a maverick slashing took out the lot, two days after an item on Radio 4 reminded us that the wayside verge is a national resource, precious for its biodiversity. A careful cut in September when seed has set – that's the schedule for this verge – but it's not what happened.

What is this place, Ghyll Brow? At the frost line the road is at its steepest pitch and embankments hide the dramatic landscape feature of the ghyll. Sheltered and inaccessible, it is a wildlife corridor. Climb clear of the trees and the wind hits you. There's wilder weather as you approach Scout Scar.

On many a March morning a woodpecker drummed in a sycamore over-hanging the road. 'Can you see it?' a passing runner called. 'Not yet,' I replied. Birdsong rose from trees deep in the ghyll where bats hibernate. It's a secret place, this ghyll whose limestone cliff plunges darkly behind the wall where spurge laurel flowers. Those snowdrops could be indigenous or thrown out from gardens, like the Spanish bluebells. Lily of the valley is native, vestigial on the verge, deep under mosses through winter.

I once saw kestrel mating here. Framed in a niche high in the barn wall, that's where the bird always sat. One summer, a fledgling scrabbled at the wall, teetered on the mossy tiles of the barn roof. Kestrel hunting along Scout Scar escarpment was a familiar sight but numbers have dropped sharply and it's several years since they bred here. There's something iconic about a barn. A vernacular building, 'ancient' said the lady who owned it and had waited eight years uncertain of its fate. Once, the barn was a store for hay and straw for the wagon horses of timber merchants with stables on Queen Street.

Each spring, those two pastures at Ghyll Brow are white with meadow saxifrage and cuckoo flower. Too steep to plough, they're a last stronghold of meadow saxifrage. Last June, Edward Chapman invited me to take a closer look. His farming regime suits them well and they depend upon it.

Ghyll Brow is a prelude to Scout Scar; its mood of pastoral and fresher air prepares the way for walkers, runners and cyclists as they leave the town behind. Its character was about to change.

March 2014, and down at Kendal Town Hall we gathered around plans and a map showing the barn and housing development to the north of Ghyll Brow, and south on those precious pastures. Here lies buried treasure, meadow saxifrage. 'I found them,' said Ivan Trimingham. So did Karen and Kevin Halcrow. So did I. Each spring we look forward to their flowering; they've earned their place in our hearts and we don't want to lose them.

Not everyone feels the same. 'It doesn't matter to me what happens here,' said one landowner eager to sell. 'I've no children.'

Retain stone walls and trees, we scribbled our suggestions on a sheet of paper beside the map. Those mature trees festooned in ivy, dripping with mosses and ferns, a roost for bats.

'Bats, you could kill the lot of them, for me.'

'Rare. Is it rare?' Lose this profusion of meadow saxifrage and it's so much rarer.

I'm taking photographs, mapping the flora and fauna of Ghyll Brow to ensure that nothing is lost simply because no one knows it's there. My map of buried treasure.

When Brunel was about to build the Clifton Suspension Bridge autumn squill would be destroyed. So the plant was relocated to St Vincent's Rocks, an inaccessible spot where it thrives today. The Ghyll Brow lily of the valley could be safeguarded in this way. I've sent photographs and grid references to Natural England and Cumbria Wildlife Trust (and a blue sock marks the spot because the plants disappear in winter). We shall see.

* Marjorie Blamey and Christopher Grey-Wilson, *The Illustrated Flora of Britain and Northern Europe*, (London: Hodder and Stoughton).

Spurge Laurel,
Daphne laureola

Meadow Saxifrage
Saxifraga granulata

Lily of the
Valley
*Convallaria
majalis*

Kendal Race Course 4

HOW FAR NOW TO KENDAL? A mile, says the milestone on the Brigsteer Road. But it's dated 1900 and change is the way of the world. Town encroaches on countryside, closer and closer.

From milestone and stile you can see Bradleyfield Allotment and the open fell leading to Scout Scar. First comes the Race Course; the outline of the track is visible and occasionally you may see a horse and rider galloping the circuit, but as a Race Course it is history.

Here is pastoral and what Brian Bowness calls 'My little Empire, my little bit of Britain.' Through binoculars, I can see the land he owns on Potter Fell. He rents the Race Course as a grazier and is tenant farmer of the pastures about Bradleyfield Farm. Here, I follow the fortunes of the farming year, a seasonal progress: tupping in October when the ewes are mated, through winter into early spring when lambing begins and the pastures about Bradleyfield Farm fill with new lambs.

A vehicle delivers feed for the flock: 'We're doing well,' says the feed rep admiring the ewes. 'We?' thinks Brian. 'I haven't seen you caring for the sheep through the winter.'

Sometimes the Race Course is a gathering place, an assembly field for sporting events. The scene is gregarious, the mood boisterous, competitive. On Boxing Day there's a traditional hound trailing meet with yelping hounds straining at the leash.

When freezing fog sweeps across the pasture it seems a bleak and lonely place.

The winter solstice is the shortest day and a time of darkness. This year I found true gold, never before and never since. Through Advent there was light: days and days of sunlight, nights and nights of

Winter Solstice 21 December 2010.

incomparable winter light, a heaven of stars and moonlight reflecting off snow and flooding the house, banishing darkness.

Long before dawn I threw open the curtains to lie in moonlight and listen to the *The Shipping Forecast*. A selenehelion: that's today's special, said the weatherman. The novelty of the word roused me to wakefulness. I put on a winter dressing gown and while the neighbourhood slept I stood in the snow marvelling at the moon and stars. The cold was fierce and the moon was low in the sky, slipping out of sight behind trees. Before sunrise, I dressed in winter walking gear and hurried to the Race Course to be on higher ground for the selenehelion: moon and sun in a word. The theme was cosmic. The shortest day was made of light, with cold from the Arctic.

Selenehelion: the winter solstice and a total lunar eclipse in a rare coincidence. The full moon sank toward the horizon in the west as the sun rose above the horizon in the east: selenehelion, a horizontal eclipse: the full-eclipse moon poised opposite the rising sun. I saw the glow of every terrestrial sunrise and sunset cast upon the moon, a swelling terracotta bite, colour of burnt earth.

Sunrise reflected off snow, warm colour illuminating the ewes crowding about the sweet-smelling haylage delivered to the feeders and packed with yellow rattle and seeding grasses. My feet ached with standing a long while in the snow in the freezing cold and I headed home for breakfast.

But now alto-cumulus was rippling across the sky so I stuffed my High Arctic wellingtons with socks, put on my duvet jacket and went once more into this rare morning.

22 March 2013   The windchill factor made it very, very cold and the fells looked iron-grey. Two days ago the track was mud. Now frozen footprints told of walkers bound for Scout Scar. There was snow in the air, a thin scatter on the ground. Newborn triplets were hurried off the Race Course and into the shelter of the lambing pens where they lay in the straw against their mother, one inert as a manky dishcloth but for a faint pulse about its rib cage. Bales of barley straw for bedding and haylage for feed stood in the open entrance to the lambing shed but nothing could keep out those easterly winds.

The coldest March weekend in fifty years saw deep snow drifts in south Cumbria, with prisoners from Haverigg helping to dig out ewes. There were heavy losses that winter and the story hit the headlines, for a while. The aftermath lingered far longer. On a cold, bright Easter Sunday, walkers bound for Scout Scar stopped for the classic photograph of snow on the distant fells and lambs in the pastures. If only life for farmers were that simple.

24 March 2014   Last winter was so cold that lambing had to be indoors, the drama of life and death hidden away in the lambing sheds.

2014 and it was mud, mud, mud through the wettest winter. But on a glorious March morning with snow on the tops there was *al fresco* lambing on the Race Course pasture. New life was enticing and the vista of snow-covered fells had to wait. On this invigorating morning newborn lambs struggled to their feet and breathed chilly air. They're so resilient when my fingers were numb with cold.

A ewe in labour pawed the ground, lay down panting, her flanks heaved with contractions, her tail wagged, she stretched upward, sky-pointing. Her lamb presented feet-first but it was coming slowly and Brian had other ewes to attend to. 'She'll be fine. Clear the slark off her nose.' And he was away across the pasture.

Close to footpath and stile, a ewe slipped her lamb easily. The newborn was drenched with birth-fluids and Brian lifted it clear of dollops of afterbirth to fresh grass where the ewe licked it clean and dry. She bore a yellow stain from October when the tup mounted her. Her udder was swollen, her back-end bloody, the umbilical cord dangling. Beneath her fleece I felt the head of her next lamb in her belly.

Black crows watched and waited. There were rich pickings; bloody afterbirth and vulnerable newborn lambs. 'One had its nose pecked off this morning.' Brian can't be everywhere, there were pregnant ewes to feed, and births to attend. The crows, the crows!

A farmer with public footpaths crossing his land has more than crows and the weather to contend with. Each year he renews his notices to advise walkers that his ewes are pregnant and any disturbance could make them abort. They're written in blood red. Keeping dogs on leads protects wildlife too. Out on the open fell there are ground-nesting birds, like skylark.

Cuckoo on Scout Scar

and Helsington Barrows

SCOUT SCAR ESCARPMENT WAS RESPLENDENT with hoary rockrose, with common rockrose, horseshoe vetch and kidney vetch thick about the cliff edge. Barrowfield Farm made haylage while the sun shone, and a tractor cut swirling patterns in a pasture below.

I sat looking down over the parkland habitat of Helsington Barrows. Redstart sang in the larch trees at my back, returning to this same territory year upon year. A cuckoo called for a moment, and fell silent. I listened to a chorus of woodland birds on a morning humid and still. Swifts and swallows appeared, feeding low and skimming the tree tops, weaving above the crown of an oak. In a flash there was my bird, out in the open in silent rapid flight. A cuckoo fly-past, raptor-like, and it was gone.

Not chance, not luck. I had been on dedicated cuckoo-watch for days and I've spent years studying their behaviour: the male's habit of choosing a vantage point on a rock or a bare branch, his powerful

2 June 2012

Hoary Rockrose
Helianthemum canum

Kidney Vetch
Anthyllis vulneraria

Common Rockrose
Helianthemum nummularium

body thrust forward to emit that resonant call, his wings resting below his up-thrust tail. An unmistakeable posture.

Passing beneath a leafy oak with spreading branches, I was startled by the oddest sound; a bird being throttled, a cuckoo with hiccups, an aberration on a theme of cuckoo. I had found the female. A visual image imprints and stays, but I find an auditory image harder to fix. 'Like bath water gurgling down a plug hole,' that's the female cuckoo, said David Attenborough on 'Tweet of the Day.' She's much less vocal than the male who calls to attract her attention, a call familiar to everyone. Well, it used to be. The cuckoo is an endangered species with a spectacular decline in numbers.

Each male has a unique call, to designate and protect his territory. That doesn't surprise me since nothing about the cuckoo is simple.

8 August 2013   So what is jizz?

It goes like this. The bird flew fast and low out of nowhere. Stealth-flight, long tail like a cuckoo. Too late, said common sense, the adult cuckoo migrates to Africa late in June. It's out of season. My bird had flown so I'd never know.

Time to look for a distraction. Small birds were feeding their young so I stayed at a respectful distance, but something drew me on. Curiosity, dogged determination, I do both of those. Something was food-begging, loud and insistent. I wandered amongst bracken and juniper, following the sound. It was a morning of mizzle and poor light. A meadow pipit flew in, bringing food for a bird with a long tail, the bird I had seen in flight. I had discovered a young cuckoo. I watched the foster parent feeding her changeling until the cuckoo plunged deeper into vegetation.

I should have trusted to jizz. I knew all along. I knew in a flash I was seeing cuckoo, that's how jizz works. No time to weigh the argument. Every cuckoo I've ever seen was caught in that flight, in that instant of recognition: the long tail and pointed wings, the dynamic of the bird. This is cuckoo territory and for years I've hoped to find evidence that they've bred successfully. Now I had it.

With heavy overnight rainfall my trousers soaked to the knees in wet grasses and bracken as I searched for my juvenile cuckoo. All was silent. In drizzle and low light the landscape looked uninspiring but I knew its secret so I stuck it out and the morning grew a little brighter.

Hearing that rasping, food-begging call again, I found my bird on a bare branch of hawthorn with a backdrop of golden grasses. A stone wall served to hide me and I snuck low and came close. I saw the length of the bird and the markings of its mantle and tail. Swallows flew overhead and the young cuckoo opened wide its gape, colour of bright blood, begging for food – any source would do. For some half-hour I watched the bird before it flew and I wandered on.

I had to return that way, I had to. Now the cuckoo was sitting on the top-stones of the wall. Long insect legs dangled from the beak of the meadow pipit as she flew in to feed it. That strident food-begging call never ceased.

If I approached too close the fledgling shuffled a little further off, a fresh perspective with each move. With its cryptic colouring the bird would disappear amongst the top-stones if I were not watching so closely. Its plumage was a soft, rippling pattern that dissolved against limestone.

In May, I had photographed the male close by. It's strange to think this is a meeting denied to the young cuckoo who will never know either parent. Everything about the cuckoo is remarkable. The more you learn, the more questions arise. This young bird can fly but it will need to build up those flight muscles before its solo migration to Africa. How does it know when to depart and where to go?

When the adult returns on spring migration it makes for this same territory, perches in these same trees. This cuckoo lineage has bred here for the last thirty years, at least. It times its arrival to coincide with the meadow pipit's return to the uplands to breed and the female cuckoo selects a number of meadow pipit nests. Once her host begins to lay, the female cuckoo must find a moment when she is away from her nest, nip in and lay a single egg of her own. She needs a ten-second interval. Scattered amongst hawthorn and juniper, hidden in tussocks of grass, the ground-nesting meadow pipit and skylark hope to rear their young. It's all so fragile, so precarious with eggs on the ground, naked nestlings on the ground. Most of us would never see them but a dog would soon sniff them out. Then it's farewell cuckoo, farewell meadow pipit, farewell skylark. They cannot tolerate disturbance. In a mild winter, their breeding season begins in late February and lasts well into August.

Once, in the Black Mountains, a birder friend found a fledgling cuckoo food-begging and we watched the meadow pipit fly in with an insect and stand on its back to reach that lurid gape. Twenty five years ago it was, and the image stays sharp in my memory. Today this is my bird, a lineage I know, and to find it for myself draws me into the secret life of the place. The closer I come the more I'm in awe of everything about the cuckoo, the marvel of the bird.

Cunswick Scar
and Cunswick Fell

6

EASTER 2014 WAS GLORIOUS. Crowns of trees rose sunlit above the escarpment, with flowers of wild cherry, wych elm and ash, buds of rowan, catkins of birch, oak and willow. Spring migrants flew in, hungry and eager to breed. A feast of insects was prepared with pollinators attracted to tree-flowers warmed by the sun. A pied flycatcher sang in an oak against a blue sky. I followed the song of a redstart through Scar Wood until I found him resplendent in breeding plumage. Redstart: fire-tail he's called, for his wand of a tail that fans out into flame. He sang to attract a mate and to reclaim last year's territory in this hanging-wood anchored in the cliff face. Chiffchaff and willow warbler sang too. From deep in holly and yew came intimate sub-song, with high piping and mystery notes. In a canopy open and full of light I was up in the tree-tops amongst the birds and flowers,

Redstart

Lapwing

drawn into the life of the wood. Spot-lights shone on nest holes in tree trunks to illuminate the drama and the fresh colours of spring. All was perfect for bird watching. Once the trees were in leaf it would be more challenging.

Scar Wood is secluded and inaccessible, a sanctuary for woodland birds. Out on Cunswick Fell ground-nesting birds are vulnerable to disturbance. Poised between display and discretion, skylarks must claim a territory, attract a mate, and avoid predation. A fleck of white gleaming amongst flowers of blue moor grass resolved into a lapwing, its black plumes stirring in the breeze. I watched the pair until a woman began to throw a ball for her dogs amongst the tussocks they favoured and I never saw the lapwing again. Curlew were calling but did not stay to breed. A male wheatear perched on a hawthorn: grey crown and mantle, black eye-mask and wings, throat and breast a warm cream. Wheatear had never looked so magnificent.

Overnight, this vision of spring vanished. Easter Monday came with a chilly, blustery wind that muffled lark song and cloud-shadow drained colour from Scar Wood and the tree-flowers disappeared. The celestial lighting-console had been switched to stand-by, the stage was bare, the life of the place subdued and hidden. If the actors were

Wheatear

Blue Moor-grass
Sesleria albicans

gone the audience might as well go home too. On a day like this you can understand why walkers might come off Cunswick Fell and say there's nothing there. The poet Paul Farley said on radio that there was not much wildlife in the Lake District. I listened again, incredulous. He had been poet-in-residence at The Wordsworth Trust in Grasmere. He was biting the hand that fed him.

Walking home via Scout Scar, I was dismayed to see a pack of dogs in high-visibility coats hunting amongst the skylarks. 'They won't touch them,' their owners said. 'They found a leveret yesterday at Appleby and didn't touch it.' Imagine six large dogs salivating over a leveret.

I was watching habitat loss and species loss, I was seeing it happen. It isn't always far off and foreign, where someone else is responsible. It's happening here and now.

In early May, bird cherry bloomed in Scar Wood. Linnets were singing, skylarks rose in song-flight and stood proud on anthills, the males' crests visible. For everything there is a season and now was the time of cowslips and early purple orchids. From deep purple, the inflorescence opens up to reveal the reddish-purple stem. Beneath a hood of petals is a lip with white landing-strip marked with raised purple spots – an invitation to pollinators seeking nectar. Early purples ran riot on Cunswick and Scout Scar in a long flowering season.

June saw the limestone escarpment of Cunswick Scar and Scout Scar yellow with hoary rock rose, common rock rose and horseshoe vetch. Out on Cunswick Fell I thought I heard a yellow hammer. I stopped still and listened, willing the bird to keep on singing. With infinite care, I crept closer. But he was unconcerned and perched in the top of a hawthorn and sang on and on. With scrub on the open fell and the hanging wood close by, the Cunswick and Scout Scar habitat should suit them but this was a first, a joyous first. I told birder David Horrabin who walks on Cunswick and Scout Scar as frequently as I do. For both of us, this is the sole yellowhammer here in years.

Swifts swept close and low over a sea of grasses as I walked below the cairn on Cunswick Fell. A young runner with her dog on a lead came out of the sun, an apparition of the goddess Diana with her hounds. They ran down a grassy track, sharing the moment and gone so swiftly they might have been creatures of myth.

Fragrant orchid was the last orchid to appear. On Scout Scar there are more anthills, the flora is more diverse and in August heather is a micro-habitat for butterflies and moths. Running north to south, Cunswick Scar flows into Scout Scar, interrupted by the Underbarrow Road which exploits a fault in the limestone. Cunswick Fell saw agricultural 'improvement' during the 1980s, with an input of nutrients and grazing by dairy cattle. To encourage diverse flora the current regime avoids fertilisers and there's mixed grazing with ewes and lambs returning in spring, and with hardy cattle. That management history underlies their differences.

A proliferation of tracks criss-crossing the fell threatens ground-nesting birds. Research shows they become accustomed to walkers or runners on a discrete footpath but that's not what is happening here. Visitor management needs thinking through. It has to be in balance with conservation and it lags far behind, a neglected element.

Early Purple Orchid
Orchis mascula

Skylark

Save the Skylark

7

'I LIKE LISTENING TO THINGS,' the child confided, her hand in mine. 'Birds singing.' My heart warmed to her. In the stillness before dawn, the house sleeping, her mother had listened to birdsong and the child at her breast had heard the dawn chorus from infancy.

It was early April and through open windows the dawn chorus swelled into rapture. In times of happiness there is joy in birdsong, in times of trouble solace.

'*Pack up your troubles in your old kit bag and smile, smile, smile.*' Head for the fells and listen to skylark. I learnt lark song with my father in childhood, and '*Pack up your troubles*' too. In commemorations of the Great War the song was back, if ever it went away.

Consider their England, the Kendal Pals, those young men and boys who went to the Western Front in 1914. They were lads from a small market-town with a river at its heart, the countryside on their doorstep, and skylark everywhere. Far from home in a landscape devastated by war, the horror of the trenches was inescapable. But sometimes, through the bombardment and the guns, they heard the skylark in soaring song-flight.

A hundred years later the skylark is in trouble, with a massive decline in numbers. It's no longer a common farmland bird so you have to go further and further to hear skylark. Walking moorland and fell, you reach a certain altitude, a habitat of grass tussocks and sedges, a solitude with skylark singing.

A century ago lark song would have been the surround-sound on Scout Scar, but not anymore. In late February 2012, there was ice on the ground and lark song. In a bleak winter scene it was a song of hope and aspiration. Those few, those precious few skylark were singing on Scout Scar. I had waited eagerly for their return and I studied the birds through the spring, I always do.

When six wooden ladder-stiles appeared along a stretch of wall I knew what it meant. The British Orienteering Championships was come to the Lake District and an event was scheduled for Sunday 6 May 2012 on Scout Scar. In less than 48 hours' time! Temporary stiles would protect the walls but would take runners right into the heart of skylark territory, lots of runners would be searching for hidden controls. Skylark and pipit are ground-nesting birds which makes them vulnerable to disturbance. The cuckoo had arrived on cue to parasitise meadow pipit nests hidden in tussocks of blue moor grass. It's intricate terrain, a good choice for orienteering in autumn and winter but not now, not in the breeding season. What could be done?

I sent an email to key officials, marked URGENT. They must have been as dismayed to receive my email as I was to see those stiles appear. They had the necessary permissions, the event was imminent but their response was swift and positive. On Saturday morning I met the controller and planner to pinpoint where the skylark were and to explain how this habitat works. On Sunday morning they had cordoned off the most sensitive area and marshals would disqualify anyone who infringed the ban. The orienteers' response was impressive. Disaster averted in the nick of time.

Orienteering has an ethos of respect for the natural world, for landscape. Planners had had to negotiate permissions with farmers, with landowners, with Natural England, The National Park and The National Trust. Any infringement and there won't be a next time and that specialist orienteering map will be useless. There are parameters: it's about enjoying sport whilst respecting wildlife.

This is skylark territory but it was managed for flora and ground-nesting birds had been overlooked. To save it, you have to know it's there. I updated my species lists and maps and submitted them to Natural England. The cuckoo, the skylark and the linnet are critically endangered species, red status, experiencing a massive drop in numbers. The meadow pipit is also in decline, amber status, a conservation concern. Time-out-of-mind they've returned to Scout Scar in the spring to breed in this discrete habitat, but their hold is tenuous and random disturbance puts them under intolerable pressure.

I looked for measures in place to protect ground-nesting birds on this Site of Special Scientific Interest and found none. Down in Kendal, all along the River Kent there are welcoming interpretative boards telling of wildlife, raising awareness. The approach to Scout Scar looks as if no one cares. A clutter of dead notices about the stile onto Kendal Race Course suggests neglect, abandonment. Worn and weathered, they're far too wordy, an ecologist friend agreed. There's no co-ordination. Each interest group posts its own notice and no one removes them as they disintegrate. There's nothing to highlight wildlife, and ground-nesting birds don't feature. They needed a champion, so when none appeared I stepped forth with skylark emblazoned on my heart. That spring, I refined the approach positive: 'listen, through the wind you can hear the skylark singing.' And the request courteous: 'keeping to paths makes a difference.' Few walkers knew skylark were here. Most responded well but we need a choir of voices in harmony, not a lone soloist. And a champion has to go home sometimes so we need information boards. 'I didn't see any notices.' Unsurprising, they're fading fast.

Then during 2013, extensive building programmes for Kendal and Ulverston were unveiled. Wide-spread concern about the impact on infrastructure and the urban environment dominated the agenda. But with urban encroachment our approach to the countryside also needed some fresh thinking and a cultural shift. My study of ground-nesting birds during spring 2012 had highlighted existing pressures. But nothing had been done. Once again I submitted species lists,

Yellow Brain
Fungus
*Tremella
mesenterica*

data, and simple, practical suggestions to the National Park, Natural England, the National Trust, Cumbria Wildlife and the South Lakeland District Council. I asked how they would prepare for change, and I kept on asking. I was a reluctant campaigner and hoped to hand over the role of champion. But I could not relinquish it until this challenge was addressed and for a long time I encountered a resolute silence. If only the conservation community would come together with a coherent vision for the future and be proactive.

How much of a problem is human disturbance to ground-nesting birds? In his radio programme *Shared Planet, Ground Nesting Birds September 2014*, presenter Monty Don asked this question of Dr Rob Lambert, tourism and environment academic at the University of Nottingham. There are challenges globally, from mountain tops to coastal environment. He continued, 'Conservation organisations seem to be running behind the surge of tourism and recreation in the countryside. There's no realisation yet that actually

Rose bedegar gall
on Dog Rose
Rosa canina.

as much money needs to be ploughed into visitor management
as into conservation work.' Scout Scar illustrates his point. Visitor
management is neglected.

Scout Scar has vistas of the Lake District Fells and the Mushroom
Shelter is a toposcope whose map invites us to identify them. But
there's nothing to tell of the escarpment, a dramatic landscape feature,
nothing to highlight the natural history of this limestone grassland. The
Mushroom Shelter suggests the interest lies some ten or twelve miles
distant. Let's tell the story of countryside in a way that encourages us
to appreciate the wildlife and habitat at our feet.

As a naturalist, I like to explore different locations across Cumbria,
different habitat. Early in 2014 I began to study how the welcome
is given, how countryside is presented when outreach is done well.
Cumbrian Contrasts had begun to take shape and this was its
genesis. My new book would be the missing welcome. I charted all my
adventures along the way in a blog on my website.

www.cumbrianaturally.co.uk

Guelder-rose berries
Viburnum opulus

Whitbarrow
and Howe Ridding Wood

8

Hallowe'en
31 October
2014

'BLUSTERY, HEAVY SHOWERS AND POSSIBLY THUNDER,' said the weather forecast. Out in the Irish Sea witches were raising a storm at Hallowe'en. Dark and dismal, it seemed a day for a writer to stay ensconced in her study. But the allure was strong so on with the waterproofs and out into the wild. Hallowe'en isn't just for kids a naturalist can play too.

An English hedgerow in late October speaks of witchcraft and I know the perfect place. Bordering Durham Bridge Wood, there was shelter from lashing rain beside shrubs crammed with ingredients to concoct a witches' brew. Trick or treat? It's a Hallowe'en spectacular, a confusion of fruits luscious and deadly; scarlet berries of guelder-rose, swags of glossy red berries of black bryony, and pink fruit splitting to reveal orange seeds amongst rosy spindle leaves.

Here was enchantment. No need to venture into the wildest weather up on Whitbarrow Fell when this woodland fringe was full of surprises. Here was a new route to explore, an ancient route. The track north became rougher and narrower with overarching trees, an overgrown BOAT (Byway Open to All Traffic) which felt like a forgotten way. Masquerading as fallen leaves, fungi swarmed amongst tree roots, deliquescent and attracting flies. In yew trees ancient as witchcraft there were fleshy red arils with toxic black seeds. For over a thousand years yew have watched over travellers on foot and with packhorses making their way along thoroughfares.

Thoroughfare: a way through. Once perhaps, but on a foul and fair day in late October Nature seemed to reclaim the place for hers.

Black Bryony,
Tamus communis

In solitude the past seems closer. Bells summoned worshippers to Sunday service. Crosthwaite Church, it must be. From high in Fellside Plantation came the chatter of fieldfare, a swell of sound from a thousand birds hidden in the trees. They flew in from the north, over pastures streaked with sunlight. I welcomed the arrival of winter thrush but scarcely found them again all winter.

As the rhythms of the natural world play out the thrill lies in uncertainty. The pattern is never quite true, there are quirks and anomalies, things go awry. There is equivocation in the witches' prophecy to Macbeth and hope is dashed; *fair is foul and foul is fair.* The Berwick witches conjure storms in the North Sea to sink the sailing ship bringing King James home to Scotland with Anne of Denmark, his bride. King James thanks God for his deliverance with votive ships, and writes his *Daemonologie* – a discussion on witchcraft and necromancy. Shakespeare echoes his new king's obsession and writes his Scottish play. There are successive witch trials in Scotland and in Denmark.

Nothing is sure. If you think each autumn certain of bearing gold you are mistaken. Gales, plunder and infestation by caterpillars strip the hedgerows and not every year is fruitful. Come too early, come too late and you miss it.

Prevailing south-westerly winds shape this Whitbarrow yew

Swinging round in a horseshoe, we looked west toward the Winster Valley, passing Broad Oak and Fell Edge Farm where the track stops. This ancient way once swept all around Whitbarrow Fell to Kendal, I was soon to learn. We climbed up to Township Allotment and the limestone ridge of Whitbarrow. As we dipped down into the Township Plantation the rain intensified and bracken glowed vibrant with colour.

A straggle of damson trees ran wild on the outskirts of Row. Wizened and rotting fruit hung amongst golden leaves, with one last damson so sweet and juicy. Squashed fruit strewed the way and late roses flowered in gardens. A ladder leant against a tree, the harvest over. It had been a good year for damsons.

'So foul and fair a day I have not seen.' Sometimes, a day of foul weather is full of good things – like this one on Whitbarrow.

The Little owl was in residence and sat on a sill, contemplative. House martins swooped about the farmhouse by the Old Toll Bar crossing the Lyth Valley and swallows perched above the Lyth Valley Arms.

Sweet Cicely had aromatic green fruit and the shrubs bordering Durham Bridge Wood were in flower. Climbers launched new shoots

26 May 2014

Guelder-rose
Viburnum opulus

into space, looping and knotting through woody shrubs to create scaffolding in the hedgerow and tiny yellow flowers hid amongst black bryony's heart-shaped leaves.

There was rain so soft it was barely perceptible, with wonderful morning cloud. Toward the west and the Winster Valley a hovering kestrel was caught in sunlight. The call of the cuckoo grew louder but the bird hid in a fringe of woodland.

In August we walked the Whitbarrow ridge on a day so wild we could barely keep upright. Blackberries were ripening and there were red berries on guelder rose but something had eaten the leaves until nothing remained but lace.

Toothwort
Lathraea squamaria

Someone had snacked on cockles and thrown the shells away. Scrape back the turf and there is debris left by medieval travellers on the route from the coast that skirted below the limestone escarpment of Whitbarrow, heading for Kendal. A time when Whitbarrow and Scout Scar were grazing for sheep and cattle and the Lyth Valley and surrounding lowland was wetland. No longer a thoroughfare, the path stops here and farm land intervenes. Howe Ridding Wood National Nature Reserve is a secluded spot, you walk in and walk out and inaccessibility gives it protection. Flora and fauna is the draw, the vistas are up at the Hervey Nature Reserve on Whitbarrow Fell. Damsons flowered where a traditional orchard of apple and damson trees was being restored. At the spring-line, green hellebore flowering about a ruined wall indicates former settlement. Our guide, Joe Murphy of Cumbria Wildlife Trust, searched woodland shade beneath coppiced hazel where parasitic toothwort tapped into its roots. Next year, I know where to seek this odd perennial.

Hollowed-out pollards decomposing in fungal rot would have given fodder for cattle and sheep. Silver-washed fritillaries over-winter beneath bark. It's coppiced for flora and Joe spoke in reverential tone of the butterflies in July in this out-of-the-way nature reserve.

In contrast, Scout Scar is within walking distance of Kendal so it's more of a challenge to protect habitat and wildlife. Vistas from the escarpment are spectacular and the horizon of Lake District fells is the immediate attraction. The diverse flora and fauna of a place is revealed in a long, slow discovery, through the seasons, over the years. Whilst studying wildlife, I learn how habitat works and where the pressures are and that's integral to the experience. There are some simple measures that would make a difference in the most sensitive zones on Scout Scar. I reflected upon site designations and resources dedicated to different reserves.

Howe Ridding Wood 9 April 2014.

Buttercups and Early Purple Orchids

Humphrey Head

9

HUMPHREY HEAD IS A FINGER-LIKE PROMONTORY of limestone grassland pointing south into Morecambe Bay. A coastal headland girt with cliffs that descend to saltmarsh and the sea. Like Scout Scar, it is designated part of the Morecambe Bay Limestones. It has a maritime influence and it's exposed – something we felt on a bright and windy afternoon in May.

22 May 2013

Arriving in unfamiliar countryside, most of us won't get it without some kind of welcome. Today, our guide was Pete Jones, Reserves Officer for Cumbria Wildlife Trust. The best way to learn, the quickest and most memorable way, is to spend a day in the company of an ecologist who is working with the local farmers and managing a reserve. This was a naturalists' field-trip so Pete Jones knew he might be tested one way or another. Offset by outcropping fragments of limestone pavement, there were massed buttercups but we were being introduced to something unusual. Here was the bulbous buttercup, sepals downturned and rooted in a swollen base. Spirals of crow garlic were unremarkable, it was not in flower. Crow garlic, wild onion, *Allium vineale*: it's a speciality around Morecambe Bay, otherwise it's rare so we were down on our knees, attentive. There was horse-shoe vetch and early purple orchid, with plantains and sedges flowering thick. 'Do you have anything really rare?' Pete was asked. He thought for a moment, then named something a botanist had found once and never again. He pointed out the hoary rock rose and the Lancastrian whitebeam coming into leaf on the limestone escarpment, both rare although Scout Scar has them too. I was interested to learn how these Morecambe Bay limestone escarpments compare and contrast. As we walked I asked Pete about the grazing regime.

Cumbria Wildlife Trust has a tenancy agreement on Humphrey Head Nature Reserve and grazing has to accommodate the needs of local farmers, so this cannot be conservation grazing as a precision management-tool. Friesian dairy cattle graze the ridge but they're not the ideal breed for the distribution of the flora of limestone grassland. Keeping clear of the cliff, their influence is restricted and they are here only in summer. Sheep graze the salt marsh below, and in times of flood they are moved up onto the ridge so numbers of stock can change dramatically to suit the farmers' requirement which may not match the needs of conservation. I'm glad I asked because he gave me insights. He spoke of Humphrey Head but as I listened I was thinking how this contrasts with Scout Scar which is my special study.

Under the aegis of Natural England and the National Trust, conservation grazing on Scout Scar and Helsington Barrows can be fine-tuned with local farmers. The cattle chosen to graze this limestone grassland are up here all year, numbers fluctuate little, and these are hardy breeds, with Welsh Blacks on Scout Scar and Galloways on Helsington Barrows. Walk venturesome along the escarpment edge and hoof-prints and cow pats show the Welsh Blacks have been there before you, so there is a greater diversity of flora and a wider distribution. I've watched this happen over the years I've been studying the place. Dark red helleborine and mountain everlasting are more widely distributed and autumn gentian is prolific. These cattle are docile beasts and I've found myself taking photographs and sensing a walker almost brushing past me, only to realise it's a Welsh Black. Sometimes a blotch of darkness in the fog resolves into a cow.

Within the last few years Galloways have been introduced onto Bradleyfield Allotment. They establish trods across the fell-side, their hooves breaking up the blue moor grass so seeds of other flowers have a chance to germinate. One summer I was hunkered down studying butterflies when a pounding of the earth came closer and I looked up to see the herd advancing in single file and I was right in their path. Nothing for it, their place, their right of way and on they came, cows, calves and bull.

'Don't cattle disturb ground-nesting birds?' an orienteer asked me. An interesting question. Cattle numbers are kept in balance with the habitat they graze. As a herd, the cattle follow the trods they create. When walkers begin to use cattle trods and let their dogs loose amongst ground-nesting birds that, unequivocally, does damage.

Land ownership, tenancies, grazing rights change. Investing in stock has to be economic for the farmer. Conservation needs long-term planning and continuity which doesn't always happen. There's also the question of what a location is managed for. The requirements of flora, of birds, of butterflies are different.

Deadly Nightshade
Atropa bella-donna

Warton Crag

HE LED US INTO THE SHADOWS, into the trees where shafts of sunlight struck the plant whose every part is poisonous: *Atropa bella-donna*, deadly nightshade. 'Do not touch,' he warned us.

Atropa bella-donna, the deadly nightshade of Warton Crag. We crowded round to take photographs, wary of this plant that loomed large. Do not touch. Like an onlooker in a Caravaggio painting witnessing something extraordinary, she stood in the trees waiting. A blaze of light fell on leaves and deep bells of flowers and her face peered out of the darkness. And there she is, caught in my photographs of *Atropa bella-donna*. We thought we knew deadly nightshade but here was something bigger and bolder than we expected.

Tony Riden showed us the secrets of the place, presenting the strange and rare. He searched amongst dead bracken until he found the fresh green fern of adder's tongue, said to be an antidote to snake bite. Dark chimney sweeper moths flitted through sunlight, their furry wings flecked with soot as if the moth had emerged from a pupa buried in ashes.

We wouldn't have found adder's tongue fern but our guide knew where to look. He interpreted the landscape, telling the hidden story, showing why this place is special; 'biodiversity is here at Warton Crag.' We were up on limestone grassland and he pointed to inten- sive agriculture in the landscape below. Nearby was the RSPB Reserve of Leighton Moss with salt marsh and mud flats out into Morecambe Bay.

There was black bryony with glossy heart-shaped leaves, with green berries and vestigial flowers. In autumn, those poisonous berries

11 June 2014

Adder's Tongue
*Ophioglossum
vulgatum*

Chimney
Sweeper
Odezia atrata

Black Bryony
Tamus communis

would be in swags of glossy red, twisting about the hedgerow.

He showed us a large spindle tree and I hope to return in autumn when its pink capsules split open to reveal poisonous orange seeds. A single visit gives only a glimpse of all there is to discover through different seasons.

Tony Riden helped design the information board which tells of target species and highlights the life-cycle of the brimstone butterfly and the pearl-bordered fritillary. There's a warm welcome, with an expectation that we respect wildlife. 'Leave only footprints and take only photographs and memories.' Not everyone has read it. 'Warton Crag is a prominent limestone hill in the Arnside and Silverdale Area of Outstanding Natural Beauty (AONB) managed for its special limestone habitats, plants and wildlife, many of which are rare and protected by law.'

Biodiversity is here. There is no complacency in this claim. Looking after sites like this takes constant hard work and vigilance. The leaflets we're given make us aware of the management that underpins conservation.

In February 2015, Countryside Officer Tony Riden talked to Kendal U3A about his work with Arnside and Silverdale AONB. His critique of what an AONB is and how site designation protects natural heritage summed up all I discovered whilst I was writing *Cumbrian Contrasts*. There's co-ordination across agencies, long-term vision, clear aims, and a management plan. AONB status supports them in their bids for funding. For effective conservation all these elements must come together.

Roman sandal and limestone wall

Smardale

A BATTERED OLD SHOE has been left behind on the Coast-to-Coast walk, Smardale Bridge to Kirkby Stephen. It's not unusual to come across lost items of walkers' gear displayed on wall or signpost.

If you are up on Smardale Fell in the guise of long-distance walker you might look across Smardale Gill and Scandal Beck to a railway viaduct constructed of sandstone quarried here. There's a disused limestone quarry with limekilns and, hidden by trees, a siding on the dismantled railway where burnt lime was loaded into railway wagons. This was the Stainmore Line and it is Heritage Railway.

From Smardale Fell. Limekilns and quarry

Smardale Fell delights me every time. In March, there's the song of curlew and skylark, and a shape in the mist might be golden plover. Late-summer birdseye primrose is so inconspicuous I'm tempted to invite walkers to come and look at the flowers but they're striding out, so I resist. The Coast-to-Coast route follows a wall composed of sandstone and of limestone rich in fossils. On a winter's day the low sun illuminates the wall as if it were a well-lit sculpture gallery, each stone offset by shadows, penetrating shadows. Here are sculptures that spring surprises. The boundary between life and death is blurred by fossils in rock encrusted with lichens whose fungal fruiting structures disperse their spores like erupting volcanoes, leaving the rock pocked and pitted with calderas. Spiders float silken webs through shadow-space and lie in wait for prey. Coral fossils resemble fronds of plants, their origin is animal. Extinct marine creatures look deceptively familiar. Shells that once housed soft gelatinous creatures may have crystalline and rock-hard centres. Contemplate geology, declares whoever built this wall. Look at these gate post, one upright of sandstone, the other of limestone. I like the living sculptures of the natural world and I know few so fine.

Each time I come here I discover something new, something infinitely old. There's a Romano-British strand to Smardale, and a fossil looks like a broken-down sandal succumbed to fungal rot and lichen swarm. In grey limestone, a fossil-blob of quartz no bigger than a fingernail resembles a plaice so tiny the fishmonger would chuck it out. Aeons of time bewilder me. I'm out of my depth in equatorial seas. The man I need is palaeontologist Professor Richard Fortey who would unravel the science, shedding light on the fossils of Smardale in lively fashion. But I expect he's busy at the Natural History Museum, writing his next book, his latest TV documentary.

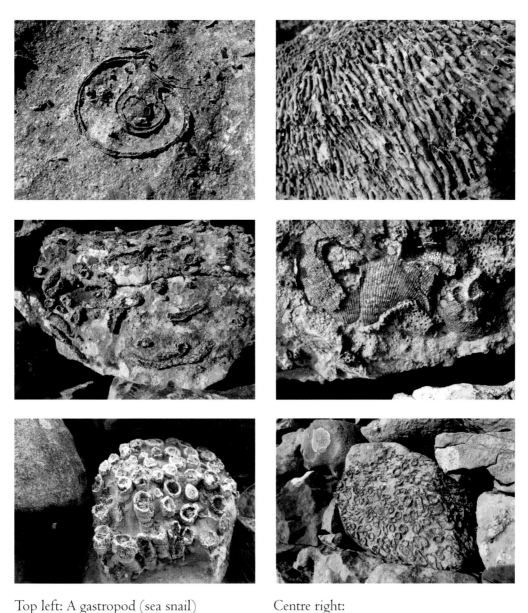

Top left: A gastropod (sea snail)

Top right: *Syringopora*
(a tabulate colonial coral)

Centre left:
Various parts of *Siphonodendron martini*
(a branching colonial coral)

Centre right:
A bivalve mollusc

Bottom left:
Siphonodendron martini

Bottom right:
Siphonodendron martini

Exploring the wall and taking photographs, the aesthetic of my image gallery has hold of me. But once I'm home, trawling through the day's catch on my computer, I want to know what I have netted. What were these marine creatures of warm and shallow equatorial seas, now translocated by seismic shift and the movement of tectonic plates to Smardale Fell? Richard Fortey's speciality is trilobites so he could bring that pale fossil-blob alive again.

Smardale meets our need to engage with landscape; setting out its geographical context, its layers of history and its ecology. There is vision in the way a welcome is presented. Smardale Gill is a National Nature Reserve and the walk follows the dismantled railway, a comfortable track which keeps clear of sensitive habitat. We walk where management wants us to go, balancing the needs of conservation with what visitors might hope to see. By the limekilns, we may read information boards on quarrying and the railway and on flora, then relax on a bench and read the landscape direct.

Smardale fifteenth-century packhorse bridge was once busy with traffic. It spans Scandal Beck, a tributary of the River Eden, whose catchment has otter, bullhead, river lamprey and white-clawed cray-fish. I might have played Pooh Sticks on Smardale Bridge when I could have been looking for lamprey. With my attention drawn to the conservation project for the River Eden catchment (SAC), I approach Smardale Bridge in a spirit of reverence.

The footpath through the Nature Reserve heads through Demesne Wood toward the railway viaduct. Wayside pictures highlight the specialities of the place; birds, butterflies and flowers. In late March blue moor grass is in flower, the food plant for the larvae of the Scotch argus butterfly. I've seen spotted flycatcher in these woods and would love to see pied flycatcher too.

Cumbria Trust for Nature Conservation affords a warm welcome. Trust is key to their relationship with visitors, of whom they have high expectations. But a flurry of admonitory notices tacked around the edges of the core display tells another story: 'no bungee-jumping off the viaduct, no abseiling, no guns, no access, no litter, it is your responsibility to remove what your dog produces and TAKE IT HOME.' Nature reserves around Cumbria echo this duality: the approach

positive weighed against an awareness of what can and does go wrong.

Like Smardale, Scout Scar is a landscape of limestone grassland with flora, butterflies and birds. They share a designation: Site of Special Scientific Interest. Special indicates global and national importance. Smardale proclaims and reiterates its distinction through a series of interpretative boards strategically located through the Reserve, Scout Scar is silent. Beside Helsington Church and at the Mushroom Shelter there are toposcopes to identify peaks in the panorama of Lake District Fells some twelve miles as the crow flies. But there are days in late May and early June when cloud masks the fells and the Scout Scar escarpment is yellow with the rare hoary rock rose. The weather can take out the fells at any season and there's not a word, not a picture to tell of treasures all about us, on the ground at our feet. Scout Scar is remarkable in itself, not merely as a window on the Lake District Fells.

One high-summer morning we cross the watershed and enter the River Eden catchment. The surrounding landscape disappears as our track dips between sunlit banks of flowers and into seclusion. Each day fresh flowers offer pollen and nectar to new broods of bees and butterflies. White wings flicker over fragrant lady's bedstraw, thyme and marjoram, and dark butterflies might be Scotch argus and Northern brown argus, if only they would settle. Their urgency contrasts with our leisure on a morning blissful as a lost Eden.

Signposts north lead up onto Crosby Garrett Fell with curlew and wild pansy, with ancient settlements and sandstone quarries.

From left:
Bloody Crane's-bill
Geranium sanguineum

Hazel
Corylus avellana, with female flower

Common Rest-harrow
Ononis repens.

A Smardale reprise through time and season

Signposts south tell of ways to Smardale Fell; ways familiar, ways for the future. In a place we love the here and now is enriched by other seasons that meld into the day and time oscillates to and fro, to and fro. Small summer birds above the railway cutting release a memory of fieldfare erupting from these bare November trees, and now winter thrush return once more.

We stop to look at the ridge and furrow field systems and the packhorse bridge over Scandal Beck, with quarries that sourced blocks of sandstone for the viaduct. And we trace our return route off Smardale Fell for later in the day. The dismantled railway now follows an embankment toward the Smardale Gill Viaduct. A railway building has door and windows bricked and boarded-up, with a perch and entrance for a barn owl cut into the wood. We hope the owl has accepted the invitation and is in residence.

At the disused limestone quarry we consider fossils in the rock face and the two limekilns. In the late seventeenth century lime mortar was needed for stone farmhouses and barns, so an interpretative board tells us. Late in the eighteenth century, burnt lime was used for arable crops and to improve pasture land. The limekilns were built in 1861, 'contemporary with the Tebay-Darlington railway line,' and supplied lime for the steelworks at Darlington and Barrow. There's a picture of a railway wagon drawn up on the siding and loaded with burnt lime and a boy who has climbed up to the draw-hole is stoking the fires. With industry silenced and gone the quarry regenerates into rock garden. We sit looking out across Smardale Gill and Scandal Beck and read of the flowers of limestone grassland, abundant on high-summer days in July, withered and gone in October. Seed-heads are capsules of story, and we have to know and love flowers to identify them from the weather-beaten autumn remnants. I like the challenge. We meet volunteers cutting back scrub and they tell of the fly orchid, revenant after an absence of thirty years and flowering once more now it sees the light. A river of herb Paris of several summers past has disappeared, overgrown with scrub but still there biding its time. 'The reserve is grazed during the winter, allowing plants to flower and set seed during the summer.' Swaledales are the management tool assisting the volunteers and we are about to meet them once more.

Small Skipper,
Thymelicus sylvestris

Scotch Argus
Erebia aethiops

Common Blue Butterflies
Polyommatus Icarus

Beyond the limekilns, our path follows the course of the dismantled railway in a gentle curve along a balcony route topped by a fence. On a mid-November day the low sun casts shadows of a ghost-railway track sweeping toward the Smardale Gill Viaduct that soars above Scandal Beck.

Amongst the hazel coppice there is dead-wood habitat; piles of decaying logs with dog lichen and mosses, a haven for invertebrates. Swaledales trot before us and, with the viaduct barred by a gate, they veer onto ground where bloody crane's-bill flowered in July. Their long tails swish as they scramble over a stone wall and onto the steep gill-side where late October gales have stripped the leaves from the trees and pools of light glimmer and die. Dark clouds scud across the sun and a squall strikes two hooded figures high on the viaduct and leaning over the railing to watch a heron flying along the beck below. The Swaledales look up in anticipation. The train is coming, they know the signal and hear it before we do: the ghost-train approaches the viaduct of a dismantled railway. Borne on a south west wind, the notes of an air-whistle grow louder. The wild wind whistles along the railings and the uprights concentrate the fluting notes like a sounding-board. It's the Smardale ghost-train and we laugh at the thrill of it. 'My great grandfather was an engine driver,' my friend declares as he tells me all about air-whistles. 'He drove trains to King's Cross and back, in the 1890s.' He ponders family lore for memories fading and almost lost.

On a sultry day in July we stand on the viaduct looking down at the white flowers of water crowfoot as Scandal Beck flows north towards its confluence with the River Eden. All is tranquil and still, the ghost-train only runs in wild weather. A hint of cloud and a breeze refreshes us but does not suit the butterflies and they vanish from the glades. Beside Demesne Wood, the berries of guelder rose are ripening and will be glossy-red in autumn, their leaves a warm rose. But something with a voracious appetite has made lace of the leaves and the gales strip every last shred from the bushes, leaving only the berries. After two poor summers there is a bumper-crop of hazel nuts, the perquisite of the red squirrel we saw in March. The Smardale wild-life would be busy caching them for the winter. I hope that's what happened because they were all gone by late October.

Dismantled railway approaching Smardale Gill Viaduct

Swaledales: from Smardale Gill Viaduct

The landscape opens up as we climb Smardale Fell and heather on Ash Fell suggests a change in geology. On a hot day the fragrance of heather moorland carried on a breeze would be ravishing.

A brood of orange-tawny butterflies forages for nectar in flowers below the fossil wall and something in the way they hold their wings stirs in my memory and says small skipper.

'Here's the pub,' I say as we reach Smardale packhorse bridge. Well, we would have found it, had we arrived some centuries earlier.

'What's for supper?' my friend asks.

'Codlings and cream – a dish of apples and cream, sweetened with honey.' Over the bridge beside Scandal Beck there is a mass of greater willow herb, its pinkish-purple flowers with a creamy centre known as codlings and cream. But with no pub there is no supper.

'Let's play Pooh-Sticks,' I suggest.

Waitby Greenriggs

From Newbiggin-on-Lune, the dismantled railway track crosses the Smardale Gill Viaduct, cuts through Smardale Gill and beneath the Smardale Viaduct (carrying trains north along the Settle to Carlisle Railway) to Waitby Greenriggs Nature Reserve. Here railways past and present intersect.

My botanist friend Fiona Holman first invited me here on a walk she was leading. Like a steward negotiating the crush in the corridor of a packed train, she went to and fro along the single track below the embankment identifying flowers on the carboniferous limestone. Choose your season and you'll find birdseye primrose, marsh helleborine, and fly orchid whose flowers resemble parachutists in full camouflage suspended beneath parachutes of green sepals. The fly orchid relies solely on insect pollination, so it mimics an insect in appearance and emits pheromones to lure the male into thinking he's found a female. Trying to mate with the flower, he transfers pollen in pseudocopulation.

Through banks of flowers the sheltered track follows the course of the former railway. Imagine the rush of turbulent air as trains passed flowers waiting for the wind to disperse their seed. The distribution of flora in these nature reserves is influenced by railways past and present. Today, careful management encourages them to thrive.

Top left:
Frog Orchid
Coeloglossum viride

Top right:
Dark Red
Helleborine
Epipactis atrorubens

Bottom left
Marsh
Helleborine
Epipactis palustris

Bottom right:
Fly Orchid
Ophrys insectifera

Dark Green Fritillary
Argynnis aglaja

Wings over Scout Scar 12

RAIN, RAIN, RAIN, FLASH FLOODS, RIVERS ON FLOOD ALERT.   *2012*
Relentless rain through April, June and late into July. The jet stream
was locked too far south, again.

After overnight rain, vegetation was lush. The morning was humid and   *5 July*
warm, an *al fresco* sauna fragrant with herbs. Shadow-wings flickered
about my shadow in an hour of bright sun. Before raindrops evapo-
rated, flowers and grasses were astir with micro-moths. Fritillaries
were everywhere, foraging for nectar and pollen, in courtship flight,
mating and egg-laying. The surround-sound was grasshoppers and
lark song. Skylark and pipit beaks were stuffed with winged insects.
Synchronicity: an abundance of insects was perfectly timed for
hungry fledglings. Skylark would soon fall silent, their breeding season
accomplished.

    Anthills were floral hotspots, their purple thyme and yellow
bird's-foot trefoil sprinkled with moths, butterflies and bees. There
was fragrant lady's bedstraw, eyebright, tormentil, fairy flax, white
bedstraws and dropwort.

    In my stillness and silence, a family of linnet came close. Kestrel
and peregrine were vocal. Young swallows twittered about the farm.

Six-spot Burnet
Moth,
*Zygaena
filipendulae*

Small Pearl-
bordered
Fritillary,
Boloria selene, on
thyme

In their short lives, six spot burnets seem to spend hours mating. A day-flying moth, their flight is a rapid whirring of wings. Black and scarlet wings spell danger and warn-off birds: a shot of histamines for meddling, anticyanins for a serious assault. Caught in the light, the scarlet hind-wing shadows veins that seem drenched with blood. Clubbed antennae are steel blue and segmented and the moth has black hairs on head and abdomen. In this burnet stronghold they were everywhere – no need to hide with those toxins.

The air was full of wings but the sky grew dark and the next downpour was imminent.

A flicker of orange, and a small pearl-bordered fritillary closed its wings and resembled a blade of grass. Close-up and broadside, its under-wing is striking and dramatic, designed to bewilder predators. Step back, and cryptic colouring works like magic as the butterfly disappears amongst flowers. A flow of dark lines traces strange asymmetries and a wash of colour smudges and blurs. Eyes are not eyes. The wing is like a medieval stained-glass window reassembled from random fragments. Contemplate the pearls, the lunulae, the intricate pattern of the under-wing, if you wish to distinguish one fritillary from another.

How to confuse predators: the question was urgent in the Great War, to protect shipping from U-boats. Impossible to hide ships at sea, instead disrupt and confuse with dazzle-ships bold in pattern and colour. The strategy was copied from camouflage in the natural world and the artist was known as a camoufleur. The evolution of butterfly camouflage is a marvel and I like the idea of a Grand Designer: the camoufleur who hides butterflies in flowers.

Scout Scar is a resource for pollinators, bees and butterflies. There's splendour in the grass on butterfly days, and when they're not on the wing there's always something to discover. Spiders draw

Common Blue, *Polyommatus Icarus,* on betony

Red-tailed Bumblebee, *Bombus lapidarius*

tall stems together to weave their nests. Filaments follow each stem of grass and a tangle of spider-silk gathers seed-heads to protect the brood. Affixed to grasses there are exuviae: the empty larval cases discarded as butterflies and moths emerge.

27 July 2014   After the glare and blaze of a heat wave, a sky with depth of cloud was a relief. The Scout Scar flora looked burnt-out and blitzed, the anthills too. Micro-moths and bees fared better in the wind than the few faded fritillaries. Heather was budding but nectar would only flow as the flowers bloomed. Carline thistle has spiny bracts guarding the florets where the red-tailed bumblebee foraged. Knapweed was a source of pollen and nectar and I followed the bees from one patch of flowers to another. Red-tailed bumblebees nest underground, at the base of dry stone walls in a colony of 50–100 bees.

   Flowers and bees need each other, theirs is a symbiotic relationship. To reproduce, flowers attract pollinators; patterns within the corolla guide them to their store of nectar, and the flowers signal with

Bumblebee with
pollen baskets

Carline thistle,
Carlina vulgaris

ultra-violet light. An electric field between flower and bee tells when the flower is out of nectar, so the foraging bee conserves vital energy – a sudden change in the weather, or running out of fuel, can be fatal.

I could hear bees buzz in spurts of sound as they approached flowers and this buzz-pollination (sonification) releases the grains of pollen. A bee feels its way into a flower, deep amongst the pollen-bearing anthers, shaking the pollen grains loose, brushing them over its soft short hairs and transferring them to the next flower it visits and pollinates. The female bee stores pollen in a corbicula (a pollen basket) on her hind legs to carry it back to the hive where pollen is fed as protein for bee larvae.

Clear, liquid nectar is also collected by bees, stored in a second stomach and transported to the hive where worker bees digest it, using enzymes to break down the complex sugars to produce raw honey which is dried and stored in honeycomb and capped with wax. Honey is an essential food source to help the colony over-winter.

The loss of pollinators was a news item on *Farming Today* next morning. Research is being funded by the manufacturers of pesticides, so there were questions surrounding transparency, openness, and accountability.

I e-mailed my Scout Scar bee-finds to 'the first ever Great British Bee Count,' a nationwide survey under the aegis of Friends of the Earth.

Swifts at sunset   I rarely set out without a camera and usually regret it if I do. So when a friend suggested an impromptu evening walk on Scout Scar it seemed like a different way of looking, and so it was.

Rippling patterns of cloud flowed from the sun: alto-cumulus mackerel sky with trails of cirrus cloud 'like a horse's tail,' she said. The Race Course was golden with seeding grasses and the low sun lit ewes and their plump lambs in a golden glow. After another hot day the evening was warm and very still. Above the escarpment, swifts screeched shrilly through the air like black scimitars as the sun sank low toward the horizon of fells. We sat at the Mushroom Shelter to watch the sunset. A man and child approached and their dog's white coat had a halo-effect as the vanishing sun under-lit effulgent cloud. I raised a bare arm to shield my eyes and motes of colour scattered through tiny hairs and I could rainbow the spectrum of light. Once the sun had dipped down below the fells we headed for home, glancing back to watch the afterglow. A row of ash trees stood in silhouette like an army on the horizon: Birnam Wood ready to march on Dunsinane.

Self-heal
Prunella vulgaris

Mallerstang Edge from Wharton Fell

Mallerstang
and East Baugh Fell

'I'M SURPRISED YOU DIDN'T GET LOST UP THERE,' the farmer from Aisgill remarked. Lost in Nordic noir, by Hell Gill, Black Moss Fell, Hangingstone Scar and Mallerstang Edge; inhospitable terrain by the sound of it. All that March day the mist hung low over High Abbotside, nor could we fathom the murder mystery we came upon.

29 March 2014

    There was only a cairn or a pile of stones to navigate by, and a fence that didn't accord with the map. New fence, old map. Through the loud wind came the song of larks on high and the bubbling call of the curlew. A wind like that should shift the mist but it did not. It might have been brewed in the Pennines, might have been pollution from sand storms in the Sahara. We heard golden plover and made them out through the glimmer. In gruff voice, red grouse flew low over peat hags and dark pools. Amongst the heather and lichens there were droppings, and here and there a soft feather. Diverse and intricate sphagna floated in quaking bog that sucked at our boots. Here is the source of the River Ure whose watershed soaks up rainfall and is reluctant to release it. Until you sink into its clutches you cannot imagine the tenacity of peat bog. It's viscous and there's nothing to push against, nothing to grasp. And if and when you're hauled to safety your bog-body feet are swathed in wads of moss and silts, your drenched garments sewn with seeds. It's an initiation that seems always to have been waiting.

It was bleak, wild and beautiful. With ground-nesting birds protected by solitude and a cloak of mist, we had the moor to ourselves, Barbara and Austin and me. At High Seat, a bluff of Mallerstang Edge loomed before us and Austin looked for a descent route. A gusty wind impelled me forward, down a steep pitch of broken ground, knees braking, braking as I went downhill and came to a halt, a trembling halt.

Aching and weary, we felt done for but our walk was nowhere near done. We fortified ourselves on fruit cake and found distractions beside the River Eden and along the way; frogspawn, saxifrage in a ditch, a gibbet of moles strung on a fence by a farmhouse. A mere dozen did not prepare us for our final find. Laid out all along the parapet of the bridge over the beck at Aisgill Farm were two hundred and forty dead moles and, using a walking pole as a measuring rod, Barbara counted them. Tiny bones pierced moleskin as they decomposed.

'They stink,' said Barbara to the farmer's son who had spent two months trapping them.

'Aye, they do. I'm going to throw them in the beck,' the lad assured her. After a life underground, death had set the moles in tunnelling posture, or perhaps it was a shovelling breast-stroke for swimming into the afterlife.

'Have you shut the gate? Walkers leave gates open, so we go round to check they're all closed at the end of the day.' Suspicion hung in the air. Blue-grey mist suffused hill and dale as lights came on in farmhouses along the fell-side.

At Hell Gill Bridge an interpretative board told of the vision behind a long-term enterprise at High Abbotside.

This Pennine moorland is a vital eco-system and its regeneration will benefit us all. There's an inference that on our watch we guard against habitat loss and species loss. Surely we have learnt from the past.

Good luck to High Abbotside. I'd like to see such commitment for Scout Scar. It makes sense to be proactive and manage for change we know is imminent, rather than stand by and witness degradation.

10 August 2014

My knees groaned remembering the descent of Mallerstang Edge, but I longed to go back. Ascent was a better choice, with a strong west wind at our backs. 'Look, there's a train coming out of the trees.' Down in the Vale of Eden, beyond the river, ran the Settle to Carlisle railway and we looked back to follow the train's journey north. Then in a final assault, feet planted firmly where we could find footholds on the steep shoulder between two gills, we crested the escarpment of Mallerstang Edge. High Seat was the high point of our route, on the border of Yorkshire and Cumbria – once this was Westmorland with the white-gold of its moorland grasses embedded in the name. Ink-wash cloud hung over us, casting gloom over the moors and unleashing sudden squalls of rain but with blue sky on the horizon the day could have gone either way. Darkness and light jostled over moody Mallerstang. The wind tore at us and if there were golden plover on this August day we did not hear them we could scarcely hear each other. Spotlights roved the millstone grit of the escarpment edge, highlighting crags, buttresses and screes.

Mallerstang
Edge

Sphagnum Moss

The marsh Forklet moss, *Dichodontium palustre*

Sphagnum Moss

Catchment was our theme. Hugh's Seat lies on the watershed, the source of three rivers; the Ure and the Swale flowing east toward the North Sea, the Eden flowing north to the Solway Firth. Above us on Black Fell Moss was Eden Springs. Life begins at the spring-head where the first flowers appear. Tough moor grass gave way to flowers of cross-leaved heath, ribbons of bog and open water, bright green sphagnum and reddish cotton grass. Mosses seemed drenched with blood and wine.

Above the crags of Raven's Nest we veered away from the edge, seeking shelter from the wind. A ruined sheep-fold snuggled into the fell-side and within its sanctuary the sun warmed us. A spring bubbled out of the ground and swallows skimmed the lichened walls of the fold where we were hidden, absorbed by the landscape, spirited away on clouds that raced across the sky.

To the west Wild Boar Fell was illuminated fitfully. Springs rose all along our High Rigg descent, through flights of curlew. 'Go back, go back,' said the red grouse as a brood tumbled out of the heather. But I was loath to leave this lonely moorland rinsed clean by the elements. The resonance of Eden Springs took hold.

At Hell Gill Bridge we joined the track heading north. *Old Road*, said the map. A shepherd found a hoard of Roman coins below Mallerstang Edge, and scrawny-shorn sheep grazed the turf amongst fragments of limestone pavement scattered like old bones. Horned Swaledales had blood-red markings as if prepared for slaughter. Vistas opened up before us along the ancient way, with Mallerstang Edge to the east and Wild Boar Fell to the west. We walked beneath a dome of blue as the afternoon grew warm and sunlit.

The Old Road is known as Lady Anne's Way. During the Civil War, in 1649, Lady Anne Clifford left her estranged husband, the Earl of Pembroke. She had lived in her husbands' great families as a river that runs through a lake without mingling any part of its streams with that lake, so she wrote. Now she headed north to claim her Clifford inheritance. She and her household travelled between her castles of Appleby, Brougham, Brough, Pendragon and Skipton in something resembling a royal progress. Crossing the River Eden, she would have noted the ruined Pendragon Castle and set about its restoration.

How do you atone for murdering an Archbishop? The shock of Thomas à Becket's assassination in Canterbury Cathedral in 1170 reverberated through Europe. Pope Alexander III canonised Becket and excommunicated the four knights who struck him down; Reginald fitzUrse, William de Tracy, Richard le Breton and Hugh de Morville, Lord of Westmorland. King Henry II had to distance himself from the knights who claimed they had done his bidding. 'Head north to Scotland. Fly south, join the Knights Templar and fight for Jerusalem.' Outcasts, far off but not forgotten. Sir Hugh de Morville had a bolt-hole in Westmorland, the newly-built Pendragon Castle was his and Hugh's Seat bears his name. His notoriety endures and the mosses below Eden Springs seem imbued with the blood of Becket and wine spilt from a chalice. If Hugh de Morville came up here to the watershed he might have pondered the different directions his story could have taken, as falling raindrops choose one of three great rivers.

In Van Dyck's portrait of the Pembroke family, Lady Anne seems isolated and disconsolate. Perhaps channelling her energies into rebuilding was her redemption. We called at St Mary's Church, Outhgill, restored by her. We passed Pendragon Castle, a ruin restored and fallen once more into ruin.

We might think the past was Paradise, was Eden, but the lives of Hugh de Morville and Lady Anne Clifford tell us Eden was lost long ago.

On Birkett Common we cooked supper and the wind grew stronger as the remnant of hurricane Bertha hit the British Isles. To the east ran the River Eden, to the west the Settle to Carlisle railway. We could see heather moorland toward Ash Fell and Smardale. 'Let's go home that way.' So we made a detour via Ash Fell Road, through the blooming heather.

23 November 2014   Up at High Dolphinsty, on a late November day when the sun broke free to illuminate cloud over Mallerstang, it looked as if the ghost-train had puffed and puffed all along the ridge leaving billowing cloud in its wake. I could make out the gills we tracked on that March descent from High Seat. The November sun showed the pattern of field walls in rare light, and the rich dark sweep of the heather marked out Ash Fell. 'Talk to me

Heather on
Ash Fell

of geology,' I asked a geologist friend, 'point out any special features,' and he did. He told of a cave in a lens of sandstone, we found coral fossils in a limestone wall and when we reached Ash Fell an information board whetted my appetite for more. This is lowland heath, rare in Cumbria. Beneath loose sediments there are underlying beds of limestone and sandstone. Intermixed with heather, there's an intricate mosaic of habitats with flora I shall save for the spring.

'To protect moorland birds DOGS ARE NOT PERMITTED ON THIS ACCESS LAND.'

*East Baugh
Fell, 19 June
2014*

Access Land does not mean anything goes. We are visitors merely. We encroach on the resident wildlife's territory. It is their place.

'Right, that's it. We don't need to walk we can stay in the car park,' said Austin on hearing the plaintive note of the golden plover I had set my heart on. And who knows, there might be merlin.

At my feet, a young grouse broke out of the heather and the whole family shot out of hiding in a clamour. We walked to the accompaniment of birdsong, skylark and pipit always, and curlew.

East Baugh Fell might seem a bleak and desolate moorland of moss, mire and syke – of Norse naming. 'Our walking group wouldn't like it,' said Barbara.

The morning was warm and still. Invasive clouds of midges set us coughing and I pulled my hat over my ears. The moor pulsed with life, hidden life that surprised us in sudden eruptions. Brown bodies scurried into tunnels that delved into grass and moss; vole, mouse, or shrew, we could not be sure, but a feast for raptors. Somewhere amongst the peat hags we heard golden plover and Austin found the bird on a bluff outlined against the sky.

Mallerstang in late March hid its secrets in a shroud of mist, not unusual in these Pennine hills. East Baugh Fell shares that sense of hidden things, wonders for the curious to discover. The flora of blanket bog threads through cushions of sphagnum among hummocks and tussocks of grass. There were drifts of bright green crowberry, its flowers even harder to find than its crow-black berries. Down amongst bilberry leaves, shreds of heather and mosses, I spied pink flowers. Cowberry or bearberry, we wondered? My camera and I delved deep. Barbara was seeking dark spots on the underside of the leaf: black cow – that's how to remember.

Bells within bells; a rich red calyx held petals fused into a pink bell with a stamen like a clapper. Cow bells, fairy cow bells set ringing when the wind blows over the moors and only the three of us to hear them. Barbara and I were lost to cowberry flowers. When we were on our feet again we found Austin had taken to drink.

Left Cowberry
Vaccinium vitis-idaea

Cranberry
Vaccinium oxycoccus

Cross-leaved Heath
Erica tetralix

Right Cloudberry
Rubus chamaemorus
flower *(top)*, leaf
(centre) and sepals
(bottom)

I've never seen such clusters of cranberry flowers as we found on the flank of East Baugh Fell. A stem infused with cranberry juice, a pendent flower with calyx of scalloped border and four pink petals. I marvel at the design and it's a well-kept secret as the plant grows in tussocky, boggy hollows that walkers tend to avoid.

I know cloudberry from Norway and in Scotland, and here it is in East Cumbria. It's a gem of the Pennines, cloudberry of upland bog and tundra whose white petals fall to leave red sepals, and that's all. Where is the fruit? Imagine trolls clamouring for cloudberry jam and throwing tantrums when they can't find the fruit to make it. Leaving their Scandinavian heartland they breakfasted on cloudberries, then stowed away on Viking longships and stuffed themselves on jam. Whoever heard of cloudberries with no fruit?

Cartmire Gill sounds a stick-in-the-mud place for troll-trouble, so from East Tarns we began a long descent beside Haskhaw Gill, tributary of the River Rawthey. We heard golden plover amongst the peat hags and found the birds sunlit and resplendent: face, breast and belly peat-hag black with a scroll of white, mantle all the golds of summer grasses. They are the rich colours of moorland, bog and tundra.

'Call that resplendent? You should see our northern race of golden plover,' the trolls sneer.

Cartmire Gill flows east to join Grisedale Beck and curlew were calling by an abandoned barn and farmstead. Green-veined white butterflies settled on rocks in the beck and pastures of buttercups were burnished with sorrel. We passed Flust and Fea Fow, Blake Mire and Mouse Syke. The northern resonance enthrals me and I should

Golden Plover

like to share the wildlife experience of the Viking settlers who farmed this landscape. If only I could. The wild boar of Wild Boar Fell are long gone and there would have been flocks of lapwing, not the lone bird we saw. And far more golden plover, although the trolls are right and the birds of Arctic breeding grounds are even smarter.

Why didn't the Vikings of East Baugh Fell keep up the tradition of writing sagas to tell their story? Maybe they did and the trolls trashed them.

Reflections

In 2014, *Tweet of the Day* presented the dawn chorus from different habitats. With a download, I can conjure High Abbotside and every heather moorland I know. I imagine a frosty night in March under the moon and stars up at Eden Springs. Out of the darkness comes a hymn to the new day, softly at first, then louder. Unseen skylark rise in song flight and curlew display in the moonlight. The plaintive call of golden plover and the redshank yodel contrast with the harsh croak of red grouse. Their music fills the darkness and the moor stirs into life.

We are the first generation to have this vicarious experience as wildlife sound-recordist Chris Watson shares his love of the natural world, the poetry in his soul, and all his science. But numbers of moorland birds are falling fast: skylark, curlew, golden plover and lapwing. Long live the dawn chorus and the conservationists at High Abbotside who seek to ensure its future.

At Hell Gill Bridge, we read of the regeneration of heather moorland, raising awareness. Grouse Moors: an important site for ground-nesting birds. That's the identity of High Abbotside. An emphasis on the country code suggests the protection of endangered species is always a challenge, even here in this remote and comparatively inaccessible location.

How do you extend a welcome whilst protecting habitat and wildlife? In nature reserves, in Pennine solitudes, where town meets countryside on Scout Scar and on the Furness Peninsula, throughout the UK, the question is urgent.

The Duddon Estuary

'UP DUDDON, THAT'S WHERE WE'D GO. I don't know where, I was only a kid.' Paddling in the river and wild daffodils, that's what Jenny remembers of family outings from Barrow.

Up Duddon became our destination on the first day of October. We shivered on the Wrynose Pass where the wind was strong and much colder than we had anticipated. So we followed Moasdale Beck toward the headwaters of the Duddon below Crinkle Crags. Cloud hugged Scafell, the becks glinted in fleeting sunlight and the ground grew rich and intricate with flames of bog asphodel and the last pink flowers of cross-leaved heath. Ribbons of open water threaded through rippling sphagnum moss. My heart sang as I knelt on cushions of moss to compose a triptych: a devotional painting for a medieval altarpiece, three glorious panels on wood. My theme was universal, the spring-head sacred through all time, the source of a river; the Duddon, the Esk, the Derwent, the Eden and the Kent, the rivers of Cumbria and all rivers everywhere. I looked up from taking

Sphagnum
Moss triptych

photographs to see my friend sprinting over the fell-side, startling the Herdwicks who scampered away into the mist and solitude. What was he doing? In the distance, he'd spotted a plastic bag in flight and was off in pursuit. Quick, quick. Gusts of wind inflated it and tumbled it along and he reached out and the wind tugged it away and on he ran in a race against litter. Got it! He waved the bright green bag in triumph, and stuffed it in his rucksack. To find litter by the sacred springs feels like a slap in the face when you're dreaming.

Blanket bog is beautiful and it's a unique habitat that we depend upon in downright practical ways. Diverse sphagnum mosses are fundamental to its ecology. They store carbon and help protect against climate change. Pollen grains deep in the peat reveal the history of climate over thousands of years, and resultant changes in vegetation. In mountain zones of high rainfall sphagnum cells sop-up and retain water and are the key to flood control. You can see how much water blanket bog holds, and how slow sphagna are to release it.

The challenge for the Environment Agency is to realise the potential of a whole river system from conservation of blanket bog on the high fells to keeping an estuary free from pollution from farming, from industry and from urban development.

Bog Asphodel
seed-head and
flower
*Narthecium
ossifragum*

Cross-leaved
Heath
Erica tetralix

Driving west beyond Grizebeck, the view suddenly opens up and the Duddon Estuary lies a hundred feet below. It's breathtaking. For years, I've loved to walk in the Dunnerdale Fells. I had resisted Cumbria's industrial heritage and wished it away, wished for an unspoilt landscape the Cistercian monks of Furness Abbey would have recognised. I remember the day when I began to see things differently, when I fell for Cumbria's coast.

Sea-fog lingered about the shore, fresh and invigorating. Inland the temperature soared. Weather and season gave the day distinction, a surreal quality. The Cistercians were working the haematite ore fields of the Furness Peninsula in the early thirteenth century although they were not the first to discover them. Theirs was open cast working with small bloomeries and forge sites. During the late nineteenth and twentieth centuries mining and iron smelting was on a huge scale and its industrial heritage appears around the Duddon Estuary in a mosaic of nature reserves that show regeneration and resilience.

23 May 2012

The Duddon Iron Works was built in the 1700s, reliant upon water power from the river and charcoal from the surrounding woods. With industry silenced, Furnace Wood was loud with birdsong and trees rose about the restored ruin of the iron works. From high on a wooden walkway we peered down into the gloom. Water had dripped and dripped to form a fringe of stalactites about an arch framing the charcoal-fired blast furnace. Ivy leaved toadflax and ferns grew in the masonry and a dusting of algae gave it a soft green hue. Lichens patterned rock, each fruit body the micro-caldera of a volcano. With the heat of charcoal and furnace long since cooled, the only explosive eruption comes from fruit-bodies ejecting their spores into the air to be borne away on the wind. Apotheca, that's what they're called. Accidental fires in the charcoal store had rendered a wall of stone igneous – a strange transmutation.

The Ancient Deer Park at Millom, read the notice in the wood. We emerged from the trees into the blazing sun and stood at Quarry View looking down to a pool streaked with green algae, down at the heart of the caldera of a large volcano. This was Ghyll Scaur Quarry and Aggregate Industries, an active working quarry and a spectacular

Common
Stork's-bill
*Erodium
cicutarium*

site. Fine-ground rock rose in sculptural mounds and a lorry tipped its load into a heap, raising a cloud of dust particles. During March 2010, the Icelandic volcano of Eyjafjallajokull began to erupt through an ice cap, ejecting a cloud of volcanic ash hazardous to aircraft engines. So the skies over Europe were shut down and, for a while, there was a profound peace. Millom Rock Park opened that year, presenting to visitors a vast caldera volcano that covered most of Cumbria 450 million years ago. The story is told with exhibits of quarried rock, and the website speaks of Aggregate Industries and Natural England working together.

We had lunch leaning against a fault line of haematite in a disused quarry site by Red Hills, with bloody cranesbill and a limestone flora to discover. At Hodbarrow Point a family was enjoying a picnic in the seclusion of a sandy cove that looked out into the estuary.

'*A million voices for nature*' reads an RSPB information board picturing bee orchid and whitethroat.

'*Because of the fragile nature of the site we request*
No vehicular access off the main by-way
No quad bike or motor bike scrambling -------'

Always and everywhere there is this undertow: a million voices for nature, but that's not everyone.

Hodbarrow Nature Reserve is a coastal lagoon surrounded

by scrub and grassland. For over a century it was the site of a large iron ore mining operation. Haematite mining ended in south Cumbria with the closure of Hodbarrow Mine in 1967. Sea-fog refreshed us and a raft of eider duck swam on the estuary. The screeching of terns grew raucous as we neared the hide at the Hodbarrow Lagoon which is a magnet for bird watchers. On spits reaching out into the water were nesting colonies of sandwich tern, common tern and little tern. In courtship ritual, a pair of sandwich tern began a long, considered approach to mating. He trod her and each time he covered her, his long and narrow wings rose skyward as he rode the wind. It was beautiful. Something spooked the colony on the spit, and they rose as one against the backdrop of ruined lighthouse and caravan-park.

Beside the River Duddon, willow and alder catkins opened to early pollinators on a warm and glimmering day when the mist lingered. Beneath the open canopy, wood anemones and wild daffodils mingled with celandines. After a morning in Dunnerdale we spent the afternoon exploring the industrial heritage of the estuary. From Haverigg, we walked to Hodbarrow Lagoon and found eider on the spit.

Easter 4 April 2015

On the Duddon Estuary is Millom Ironworks Local Nature Reserve. The ironworks closed down shortly after Hodbarrow Mine. Millom grew

Eider duck

Willow catkin

Alder catkin
male and female

from its ironworks and Norman Nicholson captures his town's loss of purpose in his poem 'On The Closing of Millom Iron Works.' '*It's a cold wind now*,' he wrote in September 1968.

Some half a century later there are skylarks singing. Only a few precious pairs but the locals don't want to lose them and I know how that feels. We followed a path constructed to take us where management wishes us to walk, overlooking a pond where natterjack toads breed. The rare natterjack is a protected species. I had never heard the mating call of natterjack toad and this could be the day. It was early April and when the fog descended again the evening would be warm and damp – the right conditions. My friend was engrossed in industrial archaeology and if I could have shown him how wild-life and industry can come together in unexpected ways he might have lingered for the novelty of it. Weeks later, I discovered a story so odd he'd have hunkered down at dusk and listened to the natter-jacks, I'm sure of it.

Natterjack toads are most particular about their breeding ponds. They like shallow pools that dry out in summer, more scrapes than pools. And they fail to thrive if the common toad invades their habitat. In consultation with Friends of the Reserve, United Utilities have invested a lot of money and thought in conservation at Millom. Their challenge is to protect habitat and wildlife whilst meeting EU targets on water quality in the Duddon Estuary. Improving the sewage system, they avoided excavation and minimised disruption by inserting new pipes into old. And they constructed new breeding ponds with 'special amphibian fencing' to protect the natterjack.

The Reserve is 'for the benefit of the local community.' Vision and aspiration are caught in a series of information boards, if we care to read them. And the culture of the place and its aims are spelled out by the Friends of Millom Ironworks Local Nature Reserve on their website.

Drawn in white on grey slate is what the RSPB hopes we will see. A lapwing stands amongst bloody cranesbill and bird's-foot trefoil and a little tern flies overhead. A horizon of fells to the north outlines Black Combe and White Combe, Scafell Pike and Coniston Old Man.

Natterjack Toad

'You are welcome to visit at any time for peaceful recreation,' declares a fun natterjack toad with all-seeing eyes. A necklace of toad spawn underlines the message as feisty skylarks define their territory, singing the bounds. This is their place through the generations and they depend upon it. Information boards name the agencies working in partnership to make all this effective. That's the way to do it – to flag-up the story underlying this achievement.

River channels meandered across the estuary to reach the Irish Sea and a few families were enjoying a late-July day on Duddon Sands. To the north rose Black Combe and White Combe, outliers of the Lake District Fells. Somewhere across the estuary lay Hodbarrow Nature Reserve, with the soft courtship calls of eider drakes in spring. In seventh-century Northumbria eider ducks found a protector in St Cuthbert. They're named Cuddy duck for their saint who revered wild-life and lived in harmony with the natural world. St Cuthbert is the saint for me. There was time for reverie and the vistas from Sandscale Haws because our guide had left for a secret location so we were resolutely looking the other way.

Sandscale Haws

He returned cradling in the palm of his hand a tiny natterjack toad, a distinguishing stripe along its back. The Duddon Estuary is an important breeding ground for this rare protected species and Reserve Manager Neil Forbes is licensed to handle them. A common lizard basked in the sun on a fence post beside a pool where natterjack toads clambered over bubbling green pondweed in a habitat constructed specially for them. There were fat, wriggling natterjack tadpoles in shallow pools in the dune slacks (the hollows between the

Cinnabar
Caterpillar
Tyria jacobaeae

dunes). Natterjacks prefer fresh water but can tolerate some salinity. On the upper shore are the temporary pools they favour, with bare sand and short vegetation for burrowing.

Neil explained the change in thinking regarding dune management. A dune system is, of its nature, dynamic and a relatively mobile system creates new habitat for new species. A stream cuts a fresh channel through the dunes and on this windy coast erosion shifts the sands, like the winter storm that dumped sand and inhibited the formation of a large reed bed.

The caterpillars of cinnabar moth were munching on ragwort, absorbing toxins, stripping the plant and keeping it in check. On our first visit six-spot burnet moths clustered on flowers of ragwort, great willow herb, thistle and thyme. Neil told of emergent broods, of timings through the spring and summer. Fielding the diverse questions our group flung at him, he was not fazed by our thoughts tacking this way and that, and all the while his eyes were on the ground, missing nothing. Ask a question and he would open it up and take it some-where revelatory.

Yellow Bird's
Nest
*Monotropa
hypopitys*

In the dune slacks he searched in creeping willow to reveal yellow bird's nest, a plant without chlorophyll, of drooping waxy flower. Its tubular-bells are translucent, wispy – their structure ill-defined. Its habit is not wholly clear. The plant has a parasitic association with a mycorrhizal fungus and its willow host. Its

appearances are erratic and unpredictable, like a ghost's. Yellow bird's nest lingers underground but its flowers may not appear each summer. For three years it was not found on Sandscale Haws. Then on the day before our return visit Neil discovered it, revenant, beneath grey willow where it lurked in hiding with the rare dune helleborine. Without our guide, we would not have found either, that's for sure.

We relished the beautiful, rare and strange. In the dune slacks there was grass of Parnassus, round-leaved wintergreen in abundance, and marsh helleborine. Neil made sure we did not overlook the exquisite strawberry clover, a creeping plant almost hidden in the grass. He told of challenges in managing this Reserve, of change from year to year, of the intricacies of Sandscale Haws with its dynamic habitats. He knows a naturalists' group will be eager to see the unfamiliar, to identify flora and to make species lists.

But sometimes there is a simpler way of being. For me, the sensation of summer 2015 was the fragrance of white clover lingering over the sunlit machair on the west coast of the Outer Hebrides. Being in clover is bliss. And when the sun shone on Sandscale Haws the dune flora gave off a heady and delicious perfume; white clover, purple thyme and yellow lady's bedstraw. To breathe the essence of summer amongst the dune flora was sublime.

Strawberry Clover *Trifolium fragiferum.*

Sandscale Haws is a gem of a place. Close to the industrial town of Barrow-in-Furness, its nature reserve is a resource for local people and for visitors and out on the dunes amidst butterflies and flowers you feel a world away from town. For a day to set the senses reeling the dune flora of Sandscale Haws will do it.

After our Easter visit to Millom Iron Works Local Nature Reserve I had read-up on the natterjack once more. They favour sand dunes and are found along the coastal strip between Barrow and Carlisle. Sandscale Haws is a natterjack stronghold and where traditional habitat has been lost the toad is being reintroduced to link-up sites and ensure a healthy

Wild Pansy
Viola tricolor

gene-pool for the species. The Millom Reserve 'has become a haven for wildlife,' perhaps the natterjack had been reintroduced. I contacted Friends to ask and what I learned from Perry Dark surprised me.

'When the Ironworks was operational there was an abundance of warm water and underground piping which made the ideal habitat.'

Urban development does not suit the natterjack but quarries and ironworks do. Imagine industry and the natterjacks thriving alongside each other with their weird mating calls bubbling out of underground piping. Underground piping: iron pipes or the song of the natterjack?

Government environmental management guidance spells out a range of prohibited activities that would disturb toads and their habitat but what if natterjacks invade and a man has to ford a river of toads to reach his garden shed, as happened at Millom? Whose habitat is this, theirs or ours? That is the question. For all our wildlife, that is the question. Ask the skylark singing the bounds if he can share with us that territory his song-flight defines as his mate lays her eggs and rears her young on the ground.

On Ascension Day, there's an ancient tradition of beating the bounds when the parish turned out to walk the boundaries together and to instil into the youngest in the community each landmark along the way, each tree, each spring. They recognised their dependence on the land and their intimate connection with it. They knew that the least infringement of their cultivation strips, the denial of access to fish in the river, to water, to firewood, could put their survival in jeopardy. Translate this for our times into water supply, food security, renewable energy sources, and sustainability. So whose is this habitat? It is an existential question.

Walney Island   Each time I pass BAE Systems at Barrow I'm reminded of what drives the economy. Nuclear powered submarines for the UK Royal Navy are designed and constructed at Barrow. Walney's off-shore windfarms

Shingle banks,
the old pier and
Piel Castle

were planned in Barrow and are monitored here. So the nature reserves of the Duddon Estuary must coexist alongside industry. We headed for South Walney and the Cistercian Way, an unfenced road beside saltmarsh and scattered with debris dumped by a high-tide. Cattle stood in our way. Slowly, slowly, they insisted, the mood here is contemplative. Behind us, Barrow glimmered in sun and mist, dissolving. Looking out toward Morecambe Bay in a silent and empty landscape we slipped into the past, conjuring how it might have been. Piel Castle loomed before us, a vista of saltmarsh, sand and mudflats. Piel Island's deep water harbour was an important port for the Cistercian monks, a refuge from storms, a defence against pirates and raids from the Scots. In 1327 the Abbot of Furness was granted licence to crenellate.

A warm and thoughtful welcome awaits at South Walney Nature Reserve. Coastguard Cottages and the car park are sheltered by shrubs where small birds twittered and swallows wove the air. There are leaflets, booklets, a sightings board showing what birds are about. In summer 2014, we chatted with the Reserve Warden about last winter's severe storms and the high-tides which make the Reserve prone to flooding, and the latest conservation project. There are picnic tables and toilets. Interpretative boards are strategically sited about the reserve, telling of history and natural history, and each hide has a display specific to its habitat and wildlife. There's every opportunity to understand the experience and put it in context.

And we were off, along the northern shore that sweeps in a curve, Piel Castle always the focus and the old pier becoming more distinct. Through the silence came the call of curlew, oystercatcher and redshank. Turnstone, greenshank and dunlin dispersed, and regrouped once we had passed by, whilst mallard fed unperturbed.

'Invaders Old and New,' declares an interpretative board. The Vikings were here. Eider duck nest on Walney and on nearby Foulney and Sheep Island. They arrived at 'their most southerly breeding location in Britain' in 1949. Nesting on the shingle banks, eider, tern and ringed plover are vulnerable to disturbance, so dogs are not permitted and visitors are asked to keep to way-marked trails and to observe from the hides. Too long, too close an interest and ground-nesting

Male eider and Shell Duck, South Walney

Seablite
Suaeda maritima

Bittersweet
Solanum dulcamara

birds may fail to thrive. They settle for predictability, it's the unexpected disturbance that spooks them.

Numbers of eider are falling because females sit tight on their nests when foxes and badgers predate, so there are six to seven males to every female. We learnt this in talking with wardens hammering in posts for an electric fence to protect the gull colony. It's not a strategy that would work for the eider because of their habit of leading their young from the nest onto the water. We had returned to see the eider drakes, distinguished by their napes of pistachio green, and their soft cooing accompanied us through the stillness of the April day.

I return to Walney Island again and again, enthralled by perspectives of Piel Castle and Walney's shingle banks with tide-mark scrawling. It's a harsh and dynamic environment, this natural sea-defence of shingle flung about by winter storms. But that bare shingle look is deceptive. Closest to sand and mudflats, comes a band of seaweed, shells of crab and whelk, a few feathers. Next is the pioneer zone of specialised flora, plants that must adapt and change their habit to survive inundation and salt spray, sinking deep roots in search of fresh water and storing it in fleshy leaves. Shingle flora clings close in a net of strands flung over sea-rounded pebbles, inconspicuous until it's beneath your feet – a strange and subtle flowering and fruiting.

In early August stems of bittersweet reached out procumbent, hugging the shingle, anchoring down. Scarlet fruit resembled net buoys, fenders for yachts, the purple calyx a rope-hold.

By mid-September bittersweet's purple flowers were gone, its

Glasswort
Salicornia

Scarlet Pimpernel
Anagallis arvensis

Viper's Bugloss
Echium vulgare

Yellow Horned-Poppy
Glaucium flavum

berries wizened. The shingle was splashed with tints of gold and beetroot juice. Dead stems of netting supported a ravel of fleshy leaves and the seed capsules of a mystery plant that might be a single species, might be several – a puzzle I shared with my botanist friend Fiona Holman as we pored over my images. 'Try annual seablite,' she suggested, 'it's very variable.' If I'd remembered the Pier Hide display I'd have known, but we like a challenge and now annual seablite is etched on my memory. 'Saltmarsh with specialised salt-tolerant pioneer plants like annual seablite, and glasswort.' In early August, annual seablite was soft green and unremarkable but I'd caught it on camera threading through strands of bittersweet.

On the approach to Pier Hide, where shingle meets mudflat and saltmarsh, I found glasswort. Wort is the Anglo-Saxon word to designate plant but glasswort resembles worms emerged from the mud in gilded, translucent wriggles. Glasswort was a burst of colour; pink, gold and green. No wonder the saltmarsh has hues of late-September rusty reds.

In grass and sand beside the track were viper's bugloss, scarlet pimpernel and dune pansy. Lovely flowers, but they did not take me by surprise, they were old friends. Dune pansy, wild pansy, heartsease, *Viola tricolor*; by any name it's exquisite.

The sound of the Irish Sea lapped the southern shore where yellow horned poppy put forth flimsy flowers that last no more than a day. Then long green seed capsules arc out, ripen and split along their length. Like a stranded octopus armed with sensory tentacles it feels summer's heat in the pebbles, senses the tang of salt in the air, and seems poised to haul up its deep tap-root and slither into the waves.

Cormorants lined the shore, dark wings outstretched like pterosaurs. I longed for a glimpse of minke whale or bottlenose dolphin out in the Irish Sea and wondered what cetaceans Viking raiders would have seen on the voyage of discovery that first brought them to this shore. Startled waders flew up in alarm, not Viking longships but only a couple of kayaks. The tide was far out, sun gleamed on the sands and a shimmering mirage rose about the wind turbines, their blades gently rotating in the least wind on another day that felt like summer even in mid-September.

Sea Hide jolted us into the twenty-first century. 'When did the wind turbines appear?' a man asked me. His timing could not have been better. After my last visit I had researched the Walney off-shore windfarms and I've rarely been so primed with engineering; it's not my forté. 'I couldn't have told you all this last week,' I concluded.

Sea Hide looks out upon wind-turbines 15 kilometres out in the Irish Sea, an important source of renewable energy. 'Natural gas is piped from the rigs in the bay across Walney to the terminal at Barrow.' Sands and mudflats are a feeding ground for thousands of birds. Dolphins and porpoise might not show but there's technology to contemplate and South Walney seeks to engage its visitors in all aspects of the environment. 'Shingle beaches build up over thousands of years, developing unusual vegetation. Vegetated shingle is scarce habitat, globally very rare.' So it's a magnet for botanists. The storms of January 2014 reshaped and moulded the spit on South Walney, but the warden told us the summer flora was exceptional.

I like the way South Walney tells its story. It's selective, it has to be, and it whets the appetite for more. I wanted to know that the impact of wind-turbines on marine life is being assessed, not only during their erection, but now.

'The wind, the wind,' said Jenny with feeling, as she remembered kids in a windswept playground when she was a headmistress on North Walney. The inclination of trees tells the way the wind blows.

At Earnse Point, sea-defences were being restored before the next winter storms. Great boulders shored-up the coastal track and the path was compacted down.

Coming to North Walney at low-tide, we walked on the sands that reached out far before us. Next time, high-tide forced us up onto the shingle banks and we found carpets of sea campion, flowers and seed heads at our feet.

Dunlin

Countryside 15

what's it worth?

'WHAT DO YOU WANT FROM TODAY'S WALK?' I asked.

'Peace,' said Gerald. 'And views opening up.' 'Exercise,' said Geoff. 'Solitude,' said Mike, 'quietude, and flowers.'

Thistledown was on the loose as silken parachutes launched on the faintest breeze into a blue sky. Late butterflies foraged on fading flowers; red admirals, peacocks and large whites. 'Do you think they were creeping thistles?' Fiona asked me. In a sea of thistles I was contemplating sunlight on silk and the release of seeds into the air. 'I've found more of your butterflies,' said Juan who gifted me all the butterflies along the Ribble Way and the Pennine Way. All day we had glimpses of Ingleborough, Pen-y-Ghent and Whernside: 'It's an iconic route,' announced Mike who was leading our walk. 'That's what they say of everything these days, iconic.' The way he tells it makes me smile.

'It's a good path isn't it?' Margaret pointed out the compacted gravels and pebbles with grass softening the look. We did not stray because it suited us, being the best route and comfortable underfoot. Something on a post caught my eye.

The Three Peaks: Yorkshire Dales
Enjoyed your walk?
Donate now towards path maintenance

Pay for a walk in the countryside. Why should we?

Well, on a September day in what seemed like an endless summer this was a memorable walk. Iconic, thanks to Mike Jackson. This pithy message makes us think. In planning a path like The Pennine Way route-choice is critical. The path must appeal to walkers, keeping us clear of sensitive habitat and the wildlife and livestock in residence, keeping us predictable. We passed Belgian Blue cows with their calves, and sheep. This is their place. Walkers tend to veer off to a vantage point, to take a shortcut. 'Desire paths,' said Dennis, 'that's what they're called.' The Pennine Way has to seem the route we would choose. And this well-made surface of compacted stone is exposed to water-erosion and hammer from walkers, so maintenance is on-going.

So what's it worth? Here's the barcode, let's make our contribution whilst the fun of the day is fresh in our minds. Quick Response Code it's called. All we need is a smartphone. Donate: let's consider what we have to give. QR suggests things to come, possibilities. That barcode connects to a website, a data source that would be easy to update and develop. 'You'd enjoy writing that,' a friend suggested. Information boards tell the story, give the welcome, the subtext and the inference. They are a well-established tradition. QR has the potential to open up the way we connect with countryside. The notice is unobtrusive and looks robust so it's less prone to vandalism. Countryside is not empty space, that's the message. We rarely meet landowners, farmers and conservationists but they're working together to plan for the future. That's what is happening here.

In his TV series, *The Making of Britain*, Andrew Marr spoke of the little ships sent to rescue the troops stranded at Dunkirk in 1940, and he remarked that eleven of them were named *Skylark*. The thought of Britain saved by a fleet of *Skylarks* is delightful. The bird is an emblem of hope, of aspiration, and it needs our help. For all our precious wildlife, what's it worth?

First published in 2016 by
Palatine Books,
Carnegie House,
Chatsworth Road
Lancaster LA1 4SL
www.palatinebooks.com

Copyright © Jan Wiltshire

All rights reserved
Unauthorised duplication contravenes existing laws

The right of Jan Wiltshire to be identified as the author of this work has been asserted in accordance with the Copyright, Designs and Patents act 1988

British Library Cataloguing-in-Publication data A catalogue record for this book is available from the British Library

Paperback ISBN 978-1-910837-03-0

Designed and typeset by Carnegie Book Production

Printed and bound by Latitude Press